HERE AND THERE IN THE GREEK NEW TESTAMENT....

With an introduction on

NEW TESTAMENT EXEGESIS

BY

Lemuel Stoughton Potwin, D.D.
Professor in Adelbert College of Western Reserve University

WIPF & STOCK · Eugene, Oregon

Wipf and Stock Publishers
199 W 8th Ave, Suite 3
Eugene, OR 97401

Here and There in the Greek New Testament....
By Potwin, Lemuel Stoughton
Softcover ISBN-13: 978-1-7252-9122-5
Hardcover ISBN-13: 978-1-7252-9121-8
eBook ISBN-13: 978-1-7252-9123-2
Publication date 11/2/2020
Previously published by Fleming H. Revell Company, 1898

This edition is a scanned facsimile of
the original edition published in 1898.

To the Memory

OF

My Dear Brother

PREFACE

THIS book is not a commentary, but offers itself as a supplement to the commentaries. Every student of the New Testament has general helps that shed an impartial, even if sometimes needless, light on every chapter. But in this age of books, when much of the reader's time is taken up in selecting what to read, it is but fair that the exegetical writer should select beforehand, and offer only what seems to him not found already in the necessarily common material of complete works. If he thinks that he has gained new light on various passages, let him be content to tell what has come to him here and there. Let him resolutely refrain from making a commentary. Otherwise what is really new and good in his work will be overlaid and hidden, or at least crowded and cramped, by what may be good but cannot be new. I have tried, in this little volume, to follow the advice now given.

A part of the book has been made by revising articles contributed to religious periodicals. Some of these articles have been changed so much as to almost prevent recognition; and I cannot suppose that my readers care enough for looking up my past work to wish for a full list of material previously published. I may say that No. I. is substantially from the Andover Review, that No. II. is partly from The Journal of Biblical Literature.

Not a few pages are taken, with changes, from the Bibliotheca Sacra.

In regard to the Introduction, I anticipate the criticism that it is not properly so called. If, however, it be found to have, as I hope it will, a value of its own, its lack of introductory and explanatory connection with what follows, will pass without much objection. It is not a treatise, nor even an essay, but simply a series of somewhat disconnected practical hints.

L. S. P.

Cleveland, O., June 1, 1897.

CONTENTS.

INTRODUCTION. PAGE.
    Hints on New Testament Exegesis - 11

DISCUSSIONS.
   I. A Point of Grammar in "Gloria in Excelsis"   49
  II. Ἐπιούσιος. Translated in the Lord's Prayer "daily" - - - 58
 III. Does the Lord's Prayer make mention of the Devil? - - - 84
 IV. Does Ἡλικία in Matthew and Luke Mean Stature or Age? - - - 105
   V. To the Sleeping Disciples - - 111
 VI. Demons - - - 113
VII. The New Testament use of ἀγαπάω and φιλέω 115
VIII. The Historical Present in the Four Gospels 127
 IX. Does the Preface to Luke's Gospel belong also to the Acts? - - - 130
   X. Christ's Descent into Hades - 137
 XI. Appointed to Eternal Life - - 145
 XII. Agrippa to Paul: Acts xxvi., 28 in the Light of Latin Idiom - - 147
XIII. Reconciliation by Self-Revelation - 152
XIV. The Meaning of "Foreknew" in Romans VIII., 29 as illustrated by John x., 27 155
 XV. Paul's Anathema - - - 159
XVI. Words Borrowed from the Latin - 162
XVII. Words Borrowed from the Hebrew and Aramaic - - - 182
XVIII. Words not found in Classical Writers 194

INDEXES.
    General Index - - - 203
    Index of Greek Words - - 213
    Index of New Testament Texts - 216

Here and There in the Greek New Testament

INTRODUCTION

HINTS ON NEW TESTAMENT EXEGESIS

In thinking of the conditions of highest success in the exegesis of the New Testament, we naturally make three divisions: 1st, The personal qualifications of the exegete; 2nd, The principles of exegesis; 3rd, The helpful methods. These divisions will often cross each other, and may lead to some repetition, though from different points of view.

§ 1. PERSONAL QUALIFICATIONS.

1. I mention first an open mind. This does not mean that one should be indifferent towards the topics of the New Testament, or without settled Christian opinions. Such a state of religious emptiness is exegetical paralysis. But the open mind implies such a quiet holding in abeyance and balancing of personal opinions and habits, of traditional and current views, that one may come to the task of interpretation with something of the freshness that belongs to a new investigation. Such questions as, What doctrine does this passage support? What sort of

sermon will grow out of it? Is it in harmony with a certain other text? Is it quite worthy of the writer? must wait till the open-minded soul catches the simple meaning before it. There is also a natural open-mindedness distinct from the impartiality of set purpose. The successful exegete is different from the successful writer, the latter being intensely executive, while the former is intensely and broadly receptive; open to every form of thinking, and every manifestation of character. There is in him a complete, and minute, even though quiet, attentiveness. Every ripple in the stream of thought leaves its mark. This openness extends also to the tone and spirit, as well as to the intellectual contents of a passage. The open mind, in its most active state, is kindled by a passion for the truth.

2. A mind sensitive to language. This means more than the ability to understand the main drift of language, and analyze its phrases. A sensitive mind appreciates shades of meaning, and takes impressions which it may not be able logically to explain. With photographic conformity it catches the moods of writers, and feels the power of their style. This delicate language-sense may be illustrated by the sense of hearing. A dull ear can hear shouts and rumblings and martial music. It is correct so far as it goes; but it cannot hear whispers, and soft, sweet tones, and gliding musical transitions. Sensitiveness to language may be the gift of genius, or the fruit of long reading and literary study, and the exercise of literary taste. This faculty is imperative in conjectural textual

criticism, but is also needed in ordinary exegesis. The absence of it is seen in mechanical explanations, in servile subjection to grammars and to the statistics of word-counting.

3. Sympathy with the writer. The New Testament was written with a religious intent. To understand it fully we must have a religious spirit. We go with the writer and put ourselves in his place. This is not in conflict with the open mind, for with open mind we get as near as possible to the writer in order to catch his thought and feeling, which together make his meaning. It is plain that an irreligious and unchristian person could never have *written* a truthful life of Christ. See the account of Christianity in the Annals of Tacitus (XV.,44) and the Letters of Pliny (X.,96). The same coldness or antipathy would warp the mind of a *reader*. Indeed it is a literary axiom that a writer, to be appreciated, must have a large measure of sympathy. "Not to sympathize is not to understand." This need of religious sympathy is emphasized by the inspiration of the writers. The reader needs the same Spirit. Further, as the New Testament has several authors, this sympathy must be individualized. The matter-of-fact Mark, the mystical John, the warm-hearted Peter, and the profound enthusiast, Paul, cannot be read well, all with the same feeling. The ideal exegete will enter into the mental states, and even the moods of each one. Here is the dramatic interest of New Testament exposition. All this is applicable, of course, to the speeches as well as writings in the

New Testament. And when we think of the sayings of Him whose pen wrote not a word of the Bible, we see that close communion with Christ is needed for the best understanding of his words. The interpreter must have spiritual insight.

4. Genuine interest in ancient and oriental life. The best interpreter will not have to force himself into the environment of earliest Christian writing. He enjoys standing in the midst of the life of Palestine, marking the hills and brooks, the sea and river, the flat-roofed houses, the grass in the ovens, the women at the handmill, all the out-door living. He enjoys the reproduction of the in-door life of the family, and the inner life of the soul in thought, opinion, education, worship. He enjoys going beyond the oriental, and taking in the philosophy of the West, and the early contact of Christianity with Greek and Roman life and society. By this glad living in the past he can help himself to think the thoughts of the New Testament writers, look with their eyes, and feel with their hearts.

5. A faculty for history. New Testament truth rests on a historical foundation. Even the book of Revelation has an historical starting-point, and seems like veiled history all the way through. The history found in the other books is fragmentary. The ideal interpreter is a restorer; fitting the fragments to each other, and supplying the gaps from outside history, or intrinsic probability, as best he may. And when he cannot do these things, he knows it.

6. A logical power that is flexible and adaptive. If the New Testament were a collection of orations, like those of Demosthenes, or a continuous treatise, there would be full scope for formal logic and rhetoric. As it is, there is, perhaps, equal, but different, need of logic. The book to be expounded is made up largely of familiar conversations, off-hand speeches, and letters. The course of thought is often abruptly broken; diverse topics are packed together; the feelings press hard on the intellect; the graces of style are unknown or ignored. The well-trained logician finds the logic elusive, but it is there; only it requires mental nimbleness to follow and seize it. Rigidity will fail. There is danger, on the other hand, that different subjects that are brought together simply by rapid speech, or condensed report, be forced into an artificial logical connection.

7. A knowledge of human nature and quick perception of its springs of action. A mere book-worm cannot be a good expositor, because the New Testament is full of human life. Characters must be understood in order to understand their language. The ancients are not statues in a gallery of art. We see them, real and living, in ourselves and our neighbors. Yet our knowledge of human nature must be broad, so that we shall not attribute nineteenth century manners to the men and women of the Bible. This is about the same as to say that the exegete must have common sense.

8. Passing from qualities to acquisitions, and assuming a liberal training and a working knowledge of Ger-

man and French, I mention first a wide knowledge of literature. This knowledge must not be confined to one or two languages, or one period. It must include different kinds of literature, not excepting the dramatic; also the productions of various types of mind, the less cultivated as well as the most highly cultivated. The early periods should be familiar, as exhibiting the most original and racy writing, the later periods as illustrating literary dependence, as well as careful polish and willful affectation. By this wide reach of experience the exegete is kept out of the rut of current expression in his own tongue, and is led to facility of translation and of catching meanings without translation. He is at home in literature in general. I speak now of literary, rather than philological knowledge.

9. A good knowledge of the Greek classics. The New Testament Greek, be it ever so familiar, is too narrow a basis for its own study. Its sources are in the earlier literature. Its etymologies go back to this. Although there are nearly 900 words, or about one-sixth of all in the New Testament, that may be called late Greek, i. e., later than Aristotle, yet these are nearly all from roots found in the classics. Of words not borrowed from Hebrew (about sixty), and Latin (about thirty), only six or seven are not from classical roots. Now there is needed for a true familiarity with New Testament Greek, a sense of past usage, because the past usage, though modified, still lives. Also in language-exposition so much depends on suggestion and impression, that the student cannot

afford to be without the hints and suggestions that come from the history, the changes, and the possibilities of his principal words. He must be at home in all Greek, especially the Greek that lies back of his New Testament. He must have a Greek feeling and taste, and to this end must know a much larger body of writing than is found in the Testament—and writing of a different character. An early and thorough philological study of select portions of the classics is to be taken for granted. We cannot know Greek just as Luke and Paul did, but our classical knowledge helps us to come as near as we may, by a different path, to what was to them native speech. They could not have philology, and did not need it. We can have it, and do need it. There is a green, crude philology that is out of place in Bible study, but the ripe fruits of mature philological habits are invaluable. It is only belated philology that is untimely and useless.

10. Some knowledge of post-classical Greek, outside of the New Testament. While the classical Greek is indispensable, the post-classical has this peculiar advantage, that it includes the writers contemporary with the New Testament authors, and thus enlarges the scope of illustrative usage. Beginning with B.C. 322, the year of the death of Aristotle, we have, before Christ:

(1) The historian Polybius (B.C. 204-122). Though so much earlier than the New Testament, he uses more than 100 of its late Greek words, including a very few borrowed from the Latin (μιλίον, κεντυρίων).

(2) Dionysius of Halicarnassus, historian and critic, who flourished 30 B. C.

(3) Diodorus Siculus, the historian who wrote 8 B.C.

After Christ we have:

(1) Plutarch, who wrote about A. D. 80. His "Lives" and his "Moralia," on account of their topics, illustrate the language of both the historical and didactic portions of the New Testament, and seem to stand nearer to it than the writings of any other secular writer. He uses about twice as many of the late New Testament words as Polybius.

(2) The "Thoughts" of the Emperor M. Aurelius Antoninus (A. D. 86-161) by their moral discussions are brought into close relation of verbal usage with the New Testament.

(3) The same may be said of the discourses of the Stoic philosopher, Epictetus, reported by his pupil Arrian. He taught about A. D. 90, in Nicopolis of Epirus.

11. Of post-classical, extra-Biblical authors there are two that have special claims. They were both of them Jews by race and religion, and contemporaries of the apostles. One of them, Philo of Alexandria, wrote about A. D. 40. He was the leader of the allegorical interpretation of the Old Testament—a method which was carried into the Christian church. Though a poor interpreter, he was a deep thinker, and devoted his life to the attempt to harmonize Jewish religion and Greek philosophy. His language, therefore, is often parallel with that of the New Testament, and sometimes bridges over the space between

the Septuagint and the New Testament. His works may almost be said to have been Christianized by the profound study of Christian scholars, through whose labors a second-hand Philo has become the common property of Christian students. The chief example of Philo's contribution to New Testament study is his use of λόγος.

The other Jew whose Greek illustrates the faith that he did not himself adopt, is the historian Josephus. He was born at Jerusalem A. D. 37 and died in Rome, where he lived and wrote after the destruction of his native city. Both Philo and Josephus made great use of the Septuagint, and thus are brought near to the evangelists and apostles, besides being their contemporaries.

12. It is too much to assume that all the body of Greek writing now referred to, from Homer to Plutarch, is so familiar as to be easy reading at sight. It must, however, be assumed as a condition of highest exegetical success that the Greek Testament itself is read with something of the ease with which we read a book in English. Does this suppose the work of exegesis to be already complete? By no means. It is ready to begin. When we hear a public speaker, we first understand what he says, and then, if necessary, ask him to explain what he means. Bishop Butler, and John Stuart Mill, Shakespeare, Milton and Lowell, and a host of other English writers require a reading knowledge of their language as a preparation for understanding even their difficulties. So a free reading knowledge of New Testament Greek is preliminary to exegesis. We must remove, as fully as

possible, the embarrassment of a foreign tongue. For example, it is no exegesis of Phil. ii. 6-8 to translate the passage in the ordinary meanings of the words. This is merely preliminary; and if one has to dig out half the words from the Lexicon, instead of recognizing them as already familiar, and being open at once to their suggestions, it is hardly preliminary—it is elementary. There can be a good exegesis from a good translation, for the right intellectual and spiritual force can work at second hand, but if the exegesis is to be worth anything as coming from Greek, it must come from a Greek that is familiar.

13. A good knowledge of the Septuagint. In itself this Old Testament version has points of interest. It is unique in ancient Greek literature as being a translation. It abounds in new words, about one-seventh of its entire vocabulary being not found earlier. It abounds in Hebrew idioms, yet it is genuine Greek. There are marked instances of deviation from Hebrew idiom, and evidences of the moulding power of the Greek sense of beauty. Its relation to the New Testament gives it a value belonging to no other Greek book. (1) It greatly enlarges verbal usage for New Testament work. E. g. ἀνδρίζω, ἐπίσκοπος, ἐκκλησία, λυτρόω, and even ζηλωτής. (2) It, in fact, created important parts of the New Testament vocabulary. E. g. ἀγάπη, ἄγγελος, διάβολος, and κύριος for Jehovah. (3) It expanded and deepened the meaning of many old words, and prepared them for New Testament service. E. g. εἰρήνη, χάρις, πίστις, ζωή, ἅγιος, ἁμαρτωλός, λόγος. One-quarter of the New Testament vocabulary is absent

from the Septuagint, and yet all the most important ethical and religious words are found in both.

14. A knowledge of Hebrew. The value of this requires no argument. It helps the New Testament student both directly and indirectly—directly by explaining the Hebraisms, e. g. ὁ κριτὴς τῆς ἀδικίας (Luke xviii. 6), τροπῆς ἀποσκίασμα (Jas. i. 17), τέκνα φωτός (Eph. v. 9); indirectly by fixing the meaning of the words of the Septuagint. The New Testament is, at various points, anchored to the Septuagint, and the Septuagint to the Hebrew, by its being a translation. Still further, that more indefinite but decisive influence of the Old Testament on the New which lies in the spirit and tone of the former, is made more clear and helpful by reading the Old Testament in its own tongue.

15. Some knowledge of Syriac. The peculiar value of this comes from the fact that the common speech of Palestine in the time of Christ was Aramaic, or ancient Jewish Syriac, akin to the Hebrew, but not Hebrew, though sometimes so called. Greek and Aramaic were used side by side, both in speaking and writing. There is some reason to think that there was once an Aramaic Gospel, now lost. The Old Syriac version of the Gospels, a manuscript of which was discovered in the convent of St. Katharine, Mt. Sinai, in 1892, was made not far from A.D. 150, and if earlier than the Old Latin, as is probable, is the earliest known version. It was made while Greek and Aramaic were both spoken in Palestine, and would naturally embody some Aramaic traditional meanings and

verbal suggestions of peculiar force. A half-century later we find a version of the whole New Testament, called the Peshitto, the authorized version of the early Syrian churches. Still further, about the same time, i. e., in the third century A. D., was made a version of the entire Old Testament, and made from the Hebrew. We have therefore a fruitful field of collateral study, recommended by its early place, its close connection with the vernacular of Palestine, and its extent over both Testaments.

16. Familiarity with the Latin versions. Foremost is the Old Latin, or the collection of Old Latin versions, dated in the second century A. D., which were revised by Jerome in the fourth century into the present Vulgate of the Roman Catholic church. The value of all very early versions is twofold, (1) in being made while the original language was vernacular, (2) in being open to the influence of tradition.

17. Some acquaintance with extra-canonical Christian and Jewish writings near New Testament times. These throw a side-light on both the language and thought of the earliest Christian writers. One of the latest-discovered examples is the "Book of the Secrets of Enoch" (Oxford, 1896). In the same class are the various "Apocalypses" and the "Didache" and the long known Epistle of Barnabas.

18. Some acquaintance with the early Greek Fathers. Their writings are not authoritative; Greek usage had changed somewhat when they wrote; their opinions colored their interpretations; but Greek was their native

tongue, and, as we who speak the English of to-day ought to understand older English better than foreigners, so ought the Greek Fathers to know older Greek better than we. We may learn something even from the changes in their Greek. It is well to look down, as well as up, the stream of usage and idiom. Of the Greek Fathers the most helpful, no doubt, is Origen, of the third century, but we need not despise those earlier, as Clement of Rome and Clement of Alexandria, and even the anonymous Clementine Homilies, falsely ascribed to the former.

19. A knowledge of the principles of textual criticism. It is not necessary that the exegete should be an expert in questions of text. The Text of Tischendorf, or of Westcott and Hort, may be taken as correct, and in case of difference an ordinary scholar can hardly hope to remove the doubt, and may safely follow either authority, but neither blindly. Clear-sightedness is needed in every direction. An intelligent following of the textual critic's discussions may lead to the true interpretation; for questions of interpretation are used by him in determining the text. See, for example, Westcott and Hort's discussion of Luke ii. 14 (N.T. II. App. p. 32 f.) It is not the exegesis of the critic alone that comes in, but that of the early readers, quoters and transcribers. In purely conjectural emendation, if a reverent prejudice ever sees fit to allow it, the exegete will have at least equal rights and responsibilities with the textual critic.

20. Familiarity with the Higher, or analytic, Criticism. The value of this Criticism to the interpreter does

not depend on the acceptance of its provisional results, so far as composite authorship is concerned, but on the minuteness and thoroughness of its investigations; historical, literary, philological and theological. When Matthew Arnold says that the Gospel of John contains partly the words of Jesus, and partly the words of an unknown "theological lecturer," we may welcome his discrimination and insight,—and draw our own conclusions. The same may be said of a much more careful and profound thinker, Dr. Wendt, author of "The Teaching of Jesus." The Old Testament has been the greatest field, thus far, for this Criticism, but the Acts has attracted the genius of Spitta ("Apostelgeschichte, ihre Quellen"), and Revelation Vischer and others. The differences and disconnections that may seem to one critic the proof of different authors, may seem to another the work of one author at different periods of life or development, or in different circumstances, or under different inspiration, or in different moods, or in possession of new material; but the differences themselves, whatever be their value to the literary dissector, are greatly important to the interpreter. In every real difference he finds a new point of light.

21. Must, then, one be a Meyer, or a Lightfoot, before he attempt to explain a book that, without explanation, is already plain enough to bring joy and salvation to the humblest mind? I hope that this Introduction will not be thought to answer in the affirmative. Great genius, or deep spiritual insight, or the acuteness of common

sense may be a substitute for many scholarly qualifications. But it is well to have an ideal. All that has now been mentioned is contributory to the best exegesis. The best exegete will cultivate these qualifications, not to mention others, if he has them, and the best students of the New Testament, in seeking help, will follow such an exegete if they can find him.

§ 2. PRINCIPLES.

1. The New Testament is *literature*, in the widest sense; is bound by its laws, and entitled to all its liberties. It is not literature in the narrower sense of being written for the ends of literary art. It is not a law-book, nor collection of technical rules. It is not an ecclesiastical book, for ceremonial use. It is a book for general reading, and written for a practical religious purpose. It is, therefore, to be interpreted on common-sense literary principles. While it is above other books, it is yet one among books— above them in scope, but like them in structure. The fact that it is a special organ of Divine revelation does not prevent its being a thoroughly human book. Questions of logic, style, origin of expressions, authorities for facts, stimulus to composition, evidence of revision, and all other literary, critical, and philological questions are as legitimate as in a book not illuminated by Divine light.

2. It is a book of the times and for the times. The times leave their mark on the mental habits, knowledge, tastes, and language of the writer, and on his views of life. Not only his single words, but his phrases and

whole conceptions are to be interpreted in the light of his training and surroundings. This does not mean that he cannot be in advance of his times, but that his writing must grow out of the times, however far they may reach above and beyond them.

3. Every New Testament writer, in every sentence that he wrote, had a meaning. We may not be able to find the meaning of every passage, but, if the text be genuine, the meaning is certainly there. This principle works in two opposite ways. It leads to the correction of the text, if correction is needed, for the text is not genuine if it has no meaning. On the other hand, it leads to earnest and manifold efforts to discover the meaning of the text as it stands.

4. The meaning is not always clear in details, even to the writer, not logically sharply defined. E. g. the expression, to be "in Christ," was probably as incapable of explicit definition to the writer as to many subsequent readers. So where feeling is chiefly concerned, the intellectual framework of the passage may be very indefinite. It requires exegetical wisdom to stop where the writer stops, and suppress the inclination to define and develop his thought.

5. We must not suppose that the writer is absorbed in *words*, and that if he changes his words he necessarily means something different. The adoption of certain words in earnest thought and rapid writing or speech, depends on causes too subtle to allow of mechanical classification long after the writing is done. A glance of the

eye on some word already written, the recollection of some word used in similar connection, the flow of the sentence, or ease of pronunciation, and innumerable other slight influences may bring a word to the tongue or pen. This is true of all times and grades of literary production, but is especially true of New Testament language, which is characterized by simplicity, and lacks the intense *word-consciousness* of modern literature, and of the most cultivated ancient literature.

6. The Holy Spirit inspired and guided the writers, but did not destroy nor veil their personal peculiarities; nor was it necessary that He should remove their personal ignorance, especially if it was shared by their immediate readers.

7. Exegesis is not philological analysis, or development. Greek etymology is a fascinating study, and is sometimes directly, perhaps always indirectly, helpful to exegesis. It may, also, be harmful by leading the mind away from simple usage and practical first impressions. E. g. συνείδησις can be understood to mean "conscience" without answering the several questions about how its etymology leads to that meaning; κόσμος in its prevailing use in the New Testament has slight dependence on the use in Homer.

8. Exegesis is not philosophical development. It may lead to the deepest problems of philosophy, as in the doctrines of Creation, Providence, and Regeneration, and in the narratives of miracles and Christian experience; it may be philosophical where the writing which it inter-

prets is such; it is greatly assisted by sound philosophy, but in itself it is quite distinct from the philosophical development of the text.

9. Exegesis is not even the same as the logical development of its text. We may infer much and well from a particular truth, e. g. from the certainty of death, but such inferences, however true and useful, are not exegesis.

10. Exegesis, or the bringing out of the meaning, is the re-statement of a writer's meaning in language that may be clearer than his own, especially to readers of our time. It is a sort of translation; not a revision; above all, not an eradication of that all-pervading element which we call, by a name unknown to the New Testament, the supernatural.

11. Exegesis is either primary or secondary. The former asks: What does the author mean in the exact form of his thought, as conditioned by his knowledge, mental state, language, times and circumstances? The latter asks: What does he mean as translated into modern forms of thought, and what is the foundation-meaning, more general and lying deeper than the primary meaning? The primary is exegesis proper; the secondary is often of more present practical value. The latter must wholly conform to the former, though it goes deeper. It is not a mere inference from the former, but is the essence of it. The primary is not simply the literal as distinguished from the figurative; it is the immediate and obvious, as distinguished from the reflective and remote. Primary exegesis emphasizes the historical, temporary and local;

secondary the general, permanent and universal. E. g., when Paul writes, "Let the women keep silence in the churches" (1 Cor. xiv. 34), primary exegesis has little to do except to show the meaning of the word "churches," but the secondary looks for the foundation-meaning in the modest deportment of Christian women in every age and every land. The distinction must be guarded from abuse, lest the secondary subvert the primary.

12. The meaning of a passage is not to be limited to the understanding of those immediately addressed. The meaning may be intentionally veiled, as when Jesus said, "Destroy this temple and in three days I will raise it up," or it may be beyond the capacity of the hearers, as when Jesus foretold to his disciples his death and resurrection.

13. Language admits of an expansion of meaning to correspond to the progress of events. Thus the expression United States of America in 1789 meant the thirteen States on the Atlantic seaboard, but in 1897 the same expression means the forty-five States stretching across the continent. So in the New Testament "all the world" when the enrollment was described meant the Roman Empire, but in the command "Go ye into all the world" the phrase looks into the future and covers the world that is there found.

14. Meaning is made up of both thought and feeling. A man means not only what he says, but what he feels, and tries almost in vain to say. If a passage culminates in feeling, it cannot be understood by a cold analysis of its logic. E. g. Rom. ix. 3, " I could wish that I myself

were accursed from Christ," is to be taken literally, but not coolly. Its literal thought is almost consumed by the fire of its feeling.

15. The general drift of a passage is the supreme authority for meaning. Words, phrases, and clauses are organized under leading thoughts and words. Words are not inflexible and independent, like blocks of wood or stone. They are more like the buds and leaves and blossoms of a tree. A word standing by itself is but a fragment of meaning. It needs its phrase and sentence that it may enter into the general aim of the writing, and thus be more truly itself, in being part of one whole. A very simple illustration of this principle is found in the words of our Savior, "The good man out of his good treasure bringeth forth good things; and the evil man out of his evil treasure bringeth forth evil things" (Matt. xii. 35), where the context demands that by "good things" and "evil things" we understand good and evil words. The principle applies closely to πᾶς and πάντες.

16. Parallel usage is either (a) imperative or permissive and alternative, according as it is uniform or varying, fixed or growing. (b) It applies to single words or to phrases, as "Son of man," "Son of God," or to whole sentences, as, "He that hath ears to hear let him hear." (c) It is traditional or original, according as its material has come down from the past, or is coined by the writer. (d) It is topical or universal, i. e., confined to certain lines of thought, or unlimited. (e) It is literal or figurative, and in comparison of passages careful discrimina-

tion should be made between them. (f) It covers different parts of speech. A verb or adjective may be parallel with a noun. Thus λογομαχέω is to be compared with λογομαχία, both words being probably coined by Paul. (g) Usage admits of various *shades* of meaning without destroying the helpfulness of the parallel. (h) It may be confined to one author, or be common to the majority of writers on the same, or kindred, subject.

17. Usage varies in value according to time. Other things being equal, first in value, outside of the writer's own pages, is contemporary usage. Second is anterior usage, as being the cause of current use. Third is subsequent usage, as being the outgrowth of earlier use. First of all is, of course, the writer's own usage, if it is sufficiently extensive. But this may vary according to his topic, his state of mind, his various surroundings.

18. Words used but once by an author, and not found in contemporary or anterior use, must have their meaning settled either by etymology, or by probable origin apart from etymology, or by the demands of the immediate context, or by comparisons with similar general thoughts, or by the probable origin of the general thought, or by the subsequent development of the word, or by the earliest versions, or by all these combined. The word ἐπιούσιος in the Lord's Prayer is a striking example of the difficulty that may attend such a word.

19. Exegesis must not confine itself to the details and minutiæ of expression. It must go beyond words, phrases, sentences, and paragraphs, and consider the

whole work, discovering, if possible, the bearing of each part on the design of the whole. It must respect the unity of the work.

20. It must not be forgotten that the one aim of interpretation is to exhibit the *power* of a writing. It is significant that the meaning of a word is often called its *force*, according to the Latin phrase *vis verborum*. To say in other language what an author has said in his own is vain, or worse, unless by removing doubt or giving a new point of view, we reveal the power of what is written.

21. Microscopic exactness does not always discover the power of a passage. E. g., it has been pointed out with great care that the word κόσμος in John i. 10 is used in three different senses. So saith the exegetical microscope; but we must forget this, and turn away from it, in order to see the power of the passage, for the one word for "world" is identified throughout.

22. *First impressions* are of great value, because they represent the natural effect of the language on the original hearer; and much of the New Testament is either the record of words *spoken*, or epistles designed to be read aloud to the assembled Christians. Of course a modern interpreter, familiar with the Bible from childhood, cannot hope for absolutely first impressions. He can, however, get *fresh* impressions, as travelers can gain new views of old landscapes, and can mark the first impressions that he receives on taking up a passage after an interval, and after unconscious preparatory experience.

For these impressions, to be worth the most, must be on a mind prepared for them. If they are sought from the Greek, the reader must beforehand know Greek well enough to get first impressions intelligently from a cursory reading.

23. When a writer does not measure his words, his reader should not. There is such a thing as an overflow of passionate utterance that ought not to be termed exaggeration. It is the natural way of expressing intense feeling. E. g. Rom. ix. 3, already quoted. We may compare the exclamation of our Savior on the cross in citing Ps. xxii. 1.

24. The principle of consistency must have a liberal application in exegesis. As between different writers, the unity of the New Testament does not require that all should write alike. James and Paul need not write alike about works and faith. Also, in different parts of the same writer's work, there may be great diversities without inconsistency. Every New Testament writer is consistent with himself, but it is his whole self, from first to last, from early all the way to late, that we are to estimate.

25. Rhetorical figures are, in general, to be interpreted as in any other book, except that we cannot hold the New Testament to the high rhetorical standard of the classics. One of the greatest errors in exegesis is confounding literal and figurative language; nor is it always easy to avoid this. The deeper the subject, the harder it is to draw the line between literal and figurative expressions.

When Jesus says, "I go that I may awake him out of sleep" (John xi. 11), no one doubts his beautiful figurative meaning; but when he says (xiv. 2), "I go to prepare a place for you," we are put upon reflection as to whether his language is literal or not. So the language applied to Christian experience, to communion with God, to the nature of God, to the unity of Christ and the church, and to the second coming, suffers such a strain of expansion that we hardly know what literary designation it deserves. Indeed it is not always necessary to determine this. We may catch the truth and power of a passage without raising any literary question whatever.

26. There is a sort of figurative force in certain commands that represent ideal attainments rather than explicit and universal directions. Dr. Maudsley, in speaking of the *failure of Christian morality*, says: "Could there be a more unhappy spectacle than that of the poor wretch who should take its moral maxims in literal earnest, and make them the strict rules of his life? The plain effects of them are to make beggars and impostors by profusion of charity; to invite affronts by easy forgiveness of injuries; to render it the interest of no one either to befriend or to forbear injuring another, because of its rigid inculcation of the same loving attitude towards friend and enemy," etc.* This failure of Christian morality should rather be called the failure of unchristian exegesis. "Whosoever smiteth thee on thy right cheek, turn to him the other also." Matt. v. 39. This means

---
*"Body and Will," pp. 167, 168.

more than face and cheeks and non-resistance; it means the heroism and self-sacrifice of love. Cheek-turning is but a symbol of heart-yearning.

27. Similes in the New Testament are either formal or informal, i. e., expanded metaphor. Example of the former: "As the lightning cometh forth from the east, and is seen even unto the west, so shall be the coming of the Son of Man." Matt. xxiv. 27. Of the latter: "What is your life? For ye are a vapor that appeareth for a little time, and then vanisheth away." Jas. iv. 14. Similes are either argumentative, or purely illustrative. Paul in 1 Cor. xv. 35-38 makes the seed sown not merely illustrative, but suggestive of the analogy between God's work in vegetable nature and in man's body. Similes of pure illustration must not be mistaken for those of argument; and similes of either kind must be interpreted according to their main point, and not pressed for minute resemblances.

28. Parables may be regarded as extended similes, and require the same caution against overpressing the particulars of the comparison. There is special danger of this, because the parable has a certain narrative or pictorial interest of its own, and therefore demands certain details independent of the lesson taught. Parables include narratives wholly, or partly, fictitious. It is not very important to determine whether a parabolic story is imaginary or not. What difference would it make, if the Prodigal Son, or the Good Samaritan, should be proved, to a certainty, to be authentic narratives of fact in every

detail? The association of either with exact names and dates might interest some readers more, but the truths taught would be the same, and the imagination of the reader might impress the truths better than the details of the biographer.

29. "Inerrancy" is a term sometimes used for a useless accuracy, or an accuracy in unimportant particulars. This accuracy, as applied to the original, but unknown, and forever unattainable, autographs, has been maintained on the ground that if the least variation from fact exists, then there may be the greatest variations and the gravest errors; for "we cannot draw the line." This reasoning is logically fallacious, and contrary to common sense—the embodiment of exegetical pettiness. As well say that if a man misspells a word he cannot be trusted to tell the truth. The New Testament may not be "inerrant" according to the standard of modern historical science, but it is not *erroneous*. The cup may have flaws, but it holds the pure water of life. Every speaker, as Stephen, delivers his *truth* to his willing hearers, and his inaccuracies, if any, to his laborious critics. It is the prime business of the interpreter to exhibit that truth; his secondary duty to examine alleged inaccuracies, estimate their value, and assign them, if proved, to their place in the necessary limitations of the writer. He need not fear them, nor make much ado over them, always remembering that *we* may be mistaken as to matters of fact, and that our most positive conclusions may be set aside by the discoveries and the critical science of the next generation.

30. Primary exegesis avoids all conflict with modern science and philosophy, because it moves on a different plane. Secondary exegesis avoids it, because it conforms to modern conditions.

31. The quotations from the Old Testament should be received in the spirit in which they are made. E. g. Matthew applies the words, "Out of Egypt did I call my son" (Matt. ii. 15), to the infant Savior. We need not trouble ourselves to prove that the nation of Israel was a type of Christ, or that Matthew was "Rabbinical" in his methods. Filled with an ardor for Christ that would see him everywhere, he saw Christ in those words, and declared that the striking and beautiful fulfillment of them was not accidental, but Divinely intended; and we may now say that He who numbers the hairs of our heads, could certainly include these words among his purposes concerning Jesus.

32. There are two ways of harmonizing seeming discrepancies in New Testament narratives: (1) by using the statements as supplements, (2) by accepting them as equivalents. E. g., for Matthew's (xiii. 55) "Is not this the carpenter's son?" and Mark's (vi. 3) "Is not this the carpenter?" Tatian's Diatessaron, the earliest known Harmony, has "Is not this the carpenter, the son of the carpenter?"*—a very simple example of harmony by supplement. Further, when Matthew says "Kingdom of Heaven" and Luke says "Kingdom of God," in reporting

---
*"The Earliest Life of Christ" (T. and T. Clark), edited by J. Hamlyn Hills; p. 112.

the very same teachings, we may accept either phrase as true, and equivalent to the other, and can hardly imagine the two Evangelists disputing over which phrase actually passed our Lord's lips. The accounts of the agony in Gethsemane furnish examples of both methods. It is not always easy to determine which method of harmonizing is to be employed; nor is it always necessary to employ either. Harmony is not identity, and harmonization is not always harmony. The highest harmony is the concord of spirit and aim. The exegete is to unfold the thought found in each of all the seemingly parallel accounts, and he gains more light from the differences than from the resemblances.

33. Traditional interpretations of the New Testament derive legitimate value from the sifting of time. They are the wheat; the chaff has disappeared. On the other hand, they may by long habit of association become so identified with the text itself, as to forestall free study. As a rule, the longer the tradition, the greater its value; but a comparatively modern tradition has the advantage of being based on a more fully developed system of study, while the earliest, as of the Greek Fathers, is based on greater familiarity with the language, and closer affinity with primitive Christian life. Times of great religious activity, as the Reformation, may start traditions of interpretation that are worthy of the highest respect. In general, traditional, like the best contemporary, opinions should be respected, even before they are weighed, and adopted, or not, *after* they are weighed.

§ 3. METHODS.

1. The Golden Rule of exegesis is, Put yourself in his place, i. e., the place of the writer or speaker, and of the original reader or hearer. Yet the mind of to-day must still be itself, while it stands in the place of the mind of the first century. The interpreter of the New Testament belongs both to the past and the present, just as an interpreter of a foreign language represents two countries. And as such an interpreter knows best his native tongue, so we must expect that the New Testament scholar will be most familiar with his own times, and will need to make special exertion to maintain his position in the past. He stands in the past to receive; in the present, to give forth what he has received. Of course there is a vast field of thought and life that is common to past and present, a field broad as human nature itself. This putting one's self in the past refers to the narrower field of the peculiarities of the past.

2. Make good use of the imagination. This is the simplest, though superficial, method of putting ourselves in another's place. Other things being equal, he will best interpret the language of our Savior in the Garden of Gethsemane, who has in his mind the fullest and most vivid picture of the scene. The imagination may be helped by reading the best books on the scenery and topography of Eastern lands. Even modern pictures are not to be despised. Personal visits will not supersede the imagination, and will fail unless they stimulate that

faculty. A view of the present may possibly blur the vision of the past.

3. More important than the imagination is sympathy. This has been already spoken of (§ 1. 3). It can be cultivated by biographical study of New Testament characters, so that we can carry a distinct impression of each one, and feel quickly the influence of events and persons upon each one. Even a certain dramatic sympathy is due to the evil characters, whose words form a part of the background of the New Testament—to Judas and Pilate and Simon Magus—as well as to Peter and John and Paul.

4. Prayer helps us to put ourselves in the place of the makers of the New Testament. I do not mean prayer without study, but prayer with study; not merely prayer for exegetical success in general, but prayer also about particular passages. Bring them into the Divine light. Pray for light on a dark text, somewhat as you pray for light on a dark path of practical duty, or for the success of a special enterprise, or for the welfare of a dear friend. Prayer brings light by communion with The Light in ways that cannot be analyzed. It is peculiarly helpful in gaining insight into spiritual truth, for it is itself within the sphere of that truth. Prayer opens our hearts to the Spirit that inspired the Scriptures. Prayer brings hope and cheerfulness in study, and rest to weariness from study.

5. Prepare for the study of a difficult passage by a systematic preliminary study of its words. This study

would include etymology, different periods of classical usage, use in the Septuagint, and in the different periods of late Greek, special emphasis being given to contemporary Greek, use in the New Testament itself, and in writing later than the New Testament and developed from it. All this to be preliminary, because if it be mixed up with the strictly exegetical work, there is danger that no room will be left for natural first impressions. It is when the words are as familiar as possible in themselves, with their various shades and alternatives of meaning, that we may expect them to show their adjustment to the connection, and to tell their own story clearly to the open mind.

6. In general, make careful study of the *great* words and phrases of the book; as ἀγάπη, πίστις, πνεῦμα, δικαιοσύνη, ζωὴ αἰώνιος; also the important ἁπαξλεγόμενα, as θεόπνευστος.

7. Study synonyms, as, βίος ζωή, ἀγαπάω φιλέω, and those prepositions that are sometimes interchangeable, remembering always the flexibility of words, the differences of writers, and the variety of usage in the same writer.

8. Look for *decisive* words and phrases, it being understood that some words are more adaptable, and dependent on connection, than others.

9. Sometimes use the side-light of another language in word-study. E. g., αἰώνιος is illustrated by its Latin analogue *aeternus*. It does not follow that the words, though analogous in origin, are identical in meaning, or have the same development, but the resemblance is no

accident, and the history of both words is the product of the same mental laws, and of similar circumstances. The usage of both is largely contemporaneous. The objections to the meaning of "everlasting," which have been brought against αἰώνιος, are equally applicable to *aeternus*, but are never seriously entertained.

10. In regard to the use of commentaries, wait till you feel your need of them. Do not begin the study of a passage by consulting them. Make them a servant rather than master. Do this although you may know that the commentator is wiser and more learned than you. Do it as the necessary means of preserving your power of independent work. Then after studying and investigating as much as you are able, take *definite questions*, if possible, to the commentary and make your own use of the answers. After your own conclusions are formed, or you have gone as far as you can independently, then test your work by the work of others, and make most of those commentaries that give reasons, and not merely conclusions.

11. Use lexicons more as repositories than as authorities. They are authorities for the reason that they are store-houses of classified usage. They are not mere glossaries. They are made from accepted texts, from concordances, and from commentaries, besides being in the line of long lexical succession. Their classifications, and meanings, and references are materials of study, and not judicial decisions, terminating study.

12. A thorough use of the Greek Concordance (Bru-

der's, or better, Moulton and Geden's, or The Englishman's, with citations in English, or Hastings', with references only) is fundamental in word-study. Yet this greatest of all outside means of study is worth little, if employed indiscriminately in piling up statistics of usage without regard to author, time, or subject. It is no substitute for separate word-study, but simply insures a view of all the matter to be studied. It is indispensable to original exegetical work. It breaks the yoke of bondage to lexicons, by admitting us to a real, though it may be humble, partnership in their work.

13. I shall not attempt to make up a book-list for the exegete, or to distinguish between those books that should be in his own library, and those that may require a short, or long, walk to reach them in the great libraries. A long list may be found in Professor Vincent's "Student's New Testament Handbook," and a more select list in Professor Thayer's "Books and their Use." Such lists are stimulating, unless they are so good and rich and full as to be paralyzing. The books that *must* lie on the writing table, or at close hand, are not many—Tischendorf's and Westcott and Hort's Texts, Liddell and Scott's and Thayer's Lexicons, a Greek concordance to the New Testament, a Septuagint, i. e., Swete's Old Testament in Greek, a concordance to the Septuagint (Hatch and Redpath's, now complete), a Hebrew Bible and Lexicon, an English Bible, Received and Revised, an English concordance, and Smith's Dictionary of the Bible. These, especially the last, will point the way to many others.

14. Passing to more general matters, I suggest the need of taking pains to break up routine and monotony. Read the passage that is under scrutiny in some foreign tongue other than the original. Better read a Choctaw Testament than keep on always in a familiar round of expression. Vary the methods of reading, now going over long passages rapidly, now slowly. Repeat a difficult passage to yourself aloud, as naturally as possible. Have passages read to you in various ways, remembering that the original writers depended mainly on hearers. Read even in various forms and sizes of type and page—anything to keep one out of a rut.

15. Learn to hold a difficult passage long in suspense, if need be; quietly waiting, at times almost forgetting, yet always keeping it where side-light from other study may fall on it, or new opportunities of direct study may solve the difficulty.

16. Read and enjoy the clear and easy passages, as stepping-stones to the more obscure; and not for stepping-stones only. Do not assume that there is nothing new to be seen in familiar texts.

17. Talk with others about your explanations; not merely with scholars, but with plain people. Either the attempt to unfold orally your thought will betray its weakness, or the excitement of interpretation face to face will give point and clearness. At any rate, one can brush away the dust that settles on too quiet solitary work.

18. Watch for favorable mental conditions. There are times when the mind is like a field-glass out of focus,

We cannot expect much then. There are moods favorable or unfavorable to clear views. Make account also of physical condition. Do not study any one passage to the point of lassitude. It may be a pleasant theory that "weak body well is changed for mind's redoubled force," but it is a very unpleasant fact that the body knows how to strike back, when the mind has wronged it.

19. Keep a list of the exegetical *problems*, e. g. 1 Cor. xi. 10, Gal. iii. 16, 20, and others, and look them over occasionally, but not too frequently, and see whether time, which means our use of time and our broadening experience, has undermined any of the difficulties.

20. Vary the points of view, in approaching a difficult passage, coming to it now as a logician, now as a poet, now as a historian, watching its response to such questions as, Is it cool or passionate? Is it dogmatic, or a meditative soliloquy? Vary the order of words, and see what the difference in meaning would be. Vary the degree and points of emphasis. Form exegetical *hypotheses*, and test them by reading, or listening to, the passage under study, and see whether they harmonize or jar. This applies especially, but not exclusively, to long passages, e. g. Christ's words about his second coming.

21. Use grammar more as a check than as a positive guide, remembering that grammar comes originally from the meaning and not the meaning from grammar. It will not do to infer that because a sentence can be put together in a certain way grammatically, therefore the meaning so elicited is respectable, or at least possible. It may not be either.

22. Try to cast off, for the nonce, your familiarity with the New Testament, and read, or hear, it as if for the first time. This is not easy; to do it perfectly is not possible; but something like it may be done by the help of the imagination. The missionary has an advantage here, in watching sympathetically the very entrance of the divine words into the minds of his converts. Every Christian parent has a similar opportunity with his young children. But without the help of social interest a mind of good literary training, in emptying itself of prejudice, in putting itself in the place of the past, can attain some of the joy and exhilaration of a new-found treasure. It can *almost* forget its knowledge and substitute discovery for memory.

23. Do not be over-anxious about the usefulness of what seems to be the meaning of a passage. The first thing is to find the *true* meaning; then the usefulness will take care of itself. The apparent sermon-producing power of a text is not always its genuine spiritual power. That is the practical aim of all good exegesis, and it comes only from the truth.

24. It is worth while to fill out by the imagination what is omitted in intentional brevity. E. g., we read in Acts xviii. 11 that Paul stayed at Corinth "a year and six months, teaching the word of God." Exegesis proper has nothing to do here, but the exegete who is filled with the spirit of his work, and is not satisfied with perfunctory explication of words, will kindle with enthusiasm at the thought of the daily life of the apostle during those eight-

een months, in the prime of his vigor and at one of the chief centers of ancient civilization. And though the interpreter, as such, is allowed no more than a passing reference to the eloquent silence of the historian, yet the habit of expanding in his own mind compressed outlines of narrative, as a microscopic picture is expanded by the magic lantern, is a noble help in interpreting all New Testament history.

25. Practice the exegesis of other authors with something of the carefulness employed on the New Testament. You will find that this is not the only book containing passages "hard to be understood"; and this fact tends to remove hard feelings, or fretfulness, in encountering obscure texts. Such study, also, gives a peculiarly valuable exegetical experience. It affords a much needed variety, breaks the monotony of style and subject, throws off any factitious solemnity, and returns the mental powers to their main task with fresh and broadened energy. Nor need this outside experience be confined to Greek and Latin. The earlier, and some of the later, English authors yield ample room. A month spent in the exegesis of Shakespeare is good preparation for a month on Paul. And if one wishes practice in Higher Criticism, Shakespeare offers a fine and harmless opportunity.

26. Be willing to accept a part, if you cannot have the whole. There is great virtue in exegetical entering-wedges. Secure every inch gained. Hold fast by every word that is settled. Look steadily in every hopeful direction of drift of thought. Work and watch and wait;

then watch and work again. Also be willing, so far as this is consistent with indomitable perseverance, to leave many things forever unexplained. This humble, but open-eyed, willingness to be left in the dark may be the forerunner of unexpected light.

DISCUSSIONS

I

A POINT OF GRAMMAR IN THE "GLORIA IN EXCELSIS"

Δόξα ἐν ὑψίστοις θεῷ καὶ ἐπὶ γῆς εἰρήνη ἐν ἀνθρώποις εὐδοκεία.
—PSALTER, Cod. A, Hymn xiv.

Δόξα ἐν ὑψίστοις θεῷ καὶ ἐπὶ γῆς εἰρήνη ἐν ἀνθρώποις εὐδοκίας.
—LUKE ii. 14.

IT is unfortunate for English-speaking and English-singing people that there is a textual difficulty in the *Gloria in Excelsis*. It makes very little difference in Greek which of the two forms given above is used. It is a matter of only one letter, and a chorus of singers need not raise a nice question of syntax on that account. But in English it makes a difference, at least in respect to clearness, whether we say and sing, "On earth peace, good-will toward men," or, with the Revised Version, "On earth peace among men in whom he is well pleased."

There is no escape, however, from the evidence that εὐδοκίας is the true reading in Luke. A clear and full discussion of the text may be found in Westcott and Hort's New Testament, vol. ii., Appendix, pp. 52-56, Am. Ed. We find there, also, as subsidiary to the settlement of the text, certain points of interpretation which will be alluded to in the following discussion. The learned editors consider the phrase ἀνθρώποις εὐδοκίας a Hebraism which would be literally translated "men of good pleasure." This is substantially the rendering of the Revised Version.

There are some objections to this construction.

1. There is the very serious objection that the meaning is not obvious. If εὐδοκία meant good-will as a moral quality, then "men of good-will," as the Rheims version has it, would be intelligible. But what does "men of good pleasure" mean? The meaning "men who are the objects of some one's good pleasure" certainly is not very natural.

2. The construction is foreign to Greek, which does not admit a "genitive of characteristic" with a personal noun, except as a predicate. Whether it is a Hebraism or not will be considered presently. It might possibly pass for a Latinism, but it goes even beyond the Latin, which does not allow this genitive without a modifying adjective—a difficulty overcome in the Vulgate by the phrase "*hominibus bonae voluntatis.*" The point is that εὐδοκίας combined with ἀνθρώποις is not genuine Greek.

3. It is not clear that the construction is a Hebraism, if it carries with it the meaning "men who are the objects of favor, or good pleasure." Cremer says (Lex., p. 215, Edin. Ed.) that if εὐδοκίας is the correct reading the phrase is to be explained like τέκνα ὀργῆς, and υἱὸς βασιλείας. But this very striking Hebraism is very different from the far simpler idiom "man of," which is perhaps as common in English as in Hebrew. We find in the

New Testament κριτὴς τῆς ἀδικίας—which certainly does not mean "judge who is the object, or victim, of injustice"—and a few other similar phrases that signify persons *possessed of* certain qualities expressed by the genitive. Neither in the New Testament nor in the Septuagint, outside of this passage, is εὐδοκίας found in combination with a personal noun that expresses the object of εὐδοκία. Such a phrase as καιρὸς εὐδοκίας in Psalm lxviii. 14 (lxix. 13), "time of favor," is quite different. What is more, the nearest Hebrew equivalent of εὐδοκία, רָצוֹן, furnishes no parallel. There is no "man of favor," although we have "day of favor" (Isa. lviii. 5), and "year of favor" (Isa. lxi. 2), which latter is quoted in Luke iv. 19, as ἐνιαυτὸν δεκτόν. The usage with חֵן appears to be the same. אֵשֶׁת חֵן (Prov. xi. 16) is translated in the Septuagint γυνὴ εὐχάριστος. In Daniel x. 11, 19, we find the original of "man greatly beloved" to be אִישׁ חֲמֻדוֹת, translated in the Vulgate *vir desideriorum*, but probably meaning "a man of charms," literally "man of precious things." Everything seems to show that the Hebraism "son of" stands by itself. To identify this with "man of" seems to be putting a grammatical—we might almost say mechanical—identity for an identity of idiom. The distinction is well illustrated by English usage, for we say "a man of wealth, of influence," etc., but not "a man of kindness (received), of anger (incurred), of caprice (inflicted)." To put the case in terms of grammar, the limiting genitive must be equivalent to an adjective, and not to a passive participle. This distinction between "son of" as meaning often "the object of," "in the condition of," and "man of" as meaning always "possessed of" certain qualities, seems to be accepted by Gesenius in the articles under בֵּן and אִישׁ. If it is valid, the basis for the interpretation "men of good pleasure" disappears.

To put the three objections into one, we may say that an over-strained Hebraism displaces a normal Greek construction and leads to an obscure meaning. Bishop Westcott, in his separate opinion (Appendix, p. 56), says well "Ἀνθρώποις εὐδοκίας is undoubtedly a difficult phrase."

I wish now to show that εὐδοκίας modifies directly εἰρήνη instead of ἀνθρώποις, and is itself modified by the phrase ἐν ἀνθρώποις. The literal translation would be "and on earth peace, [the peace] of good-pleasure in men," i. e., the peace that comes from favor, good-will, towards men.

In support of this I offer:

1. The ἐν ἀνθρώποις εὐδοκία of the early Greek Psalters. The Biblical Codex Alexandrinus, assigned to the fifth century, contains the Gloria placed at the head of this discussion. The whole hymn—Morning Hymn, Ὕμνος ἑωθινός—may be found in Swete's "Old Testament in Greek," Vol. III., p. 810. It is mostly the "Gloria in Excelsis" of our modern hymn-books, but this is followed by five lines borrowed by, or at least belonging to, the Te Deum, lines containing the only matter specially appropriate to morning:—

καταξίωσον, κύριε, καὶ τὴν ἡμέραν ταύτην
ἀναμαρτήτους φυλαχθῆναι ἡμᾶς,

and by thirteen lines from Bible sources. There is some advantage in coming to the Gloria of Luke by way of the Psalter. Here we find—dropping the Egyptian peculiarity of -εία for -ία—εὐδοκία. It is granted that this nominative case is not entitled to a place in the text of Luke, but, even if it is a corruption of Luke's text, it is genuine Greek, with a respectable history of its own, and a right to a fair interpretation. What, then, does ἐν ἀνθρώποις εὐδοκία mean in the Psalter? I cannot doubt that it means "good pleasure in men." This meaning is maintained by Cremer, on the supposition of its being the true reading in Luke, but doubted by Westcott and Hort. It is favored—

(*a*) By the combination of ἐν with εὐδοκέω in the accounts of the baptism: ἐν σοὶ εὐδόκησα, Mark i. 11, Luke iii. 22; ἐν ᾧ ηὐδόκησα, Matt. iii. 17; also of the transfiguration, Matt. xvii. 5. The other similar examples in the New Testament are οὐκ ἐν τοῖς πλείοσιν αὐτῶν εὐδόκησεν ὁ θεός, 1 Cor. x. 5, and (of things instead of persons) διὸ εὐδοκῶ ἐν ἀσθενείαις, ἐν ὕβρεσιν, κ. τ. λ., 2 Cor. xii. 10. Examples in the Septuagint are ὅτι ηὐδόκησεν ἐν ἐμοί, 2 Kings (2 Sam.) xxii. 20, and οὐκ εὐδοκεῖ ἡ ψυχή μου ἐν αὐτῷ, Hab. ii. 4, cited in Heb. x. 38.

(*b*) The order of words, which Westcott and Hort consider "unaccountable," might certainly be in prose εὐδοκία ἐν ἀνθρώποις; but in a lyrical outburst like this would not the order with εὐδοκία last be not only allowable, but more forcible?

(*c*) The absence of examples of the *substantive* εὐδοκία used with ἐν and the dative, which seems to us the only weak point in this interpretation, may be met by the general principle that verbal nouns imitate the construction of their verbs. We have examples enough of their governing the dative even without a preposition. The following are instances in the New Testament: εἰς διαχονίαν τοῖς ἁγίοις, 1 Cor. xvi. 15; διὰ πολλῶν εὐχαριστιῶν τῷ θεῷ, 2 Cor. ix. 12.

(*d*) This interpretation allows a natural division of the song into two clauses. A division into three clauses is hardly admissible, but would result from understanding ἐν ἀνθρώποις locally, "among men." In the twofold division each part would have three subdivisions. Changing the place of δόξα, to facilitate comparison, we have

| ἐν ὑψίστοις | δόξα | θεῷ |
| καὶ ἐπὶ γῆς | εἰρήνη | ἐν ἀνθρώποις εὐδοκία. |

A verbally exact parallel would give at the end of the second clause simply ἀνθρώποις—"On high glory to God, On earth peace to men,"—but instead of peace to men we have a larger thought which includes this, namely, the peace that comes from the divine favor towards men, reconciliation with men. No connective is needed before ἐν ἀνθρώποις because this phrase is appositive and explanatory of εἰρήνη; the same thought that we sing, with amplification, in the lines:

> "Peace on earth, and mercy mild,
> God and sinners reconciled."

All this in interpretation not of Luke ii. 14, directly, but of a part of Hymn xiv. of the ancient Psalter. Let us now make use of this in explaining Luke.

2. The phrase ἐν ἀνθρώποις εὐδοκίας in Luke ii. 14 should be combined in the same manner as the corresponding phrase in the Psalter. Several considerations point to this.

(a) The genitive case, found here instead of a nominative, gives a different grammatical connection for the phrase as a whole, but does not invalidate any of the reasons just brought forward in the case of the Psalter in regard to the meaning of the phrase itself. It merely offers us another possible construction, namely, as a genitive limiting ἀνθρώποις only, the objections to which have been already considered (p. 50).

(b) If the εὐδοκία of the Psalter arose from a scribe's error in copying Luke, the error would be more likely to take place if the construction with ἐν ἀνθρώποις were understood to be the same. Constructions so different as "among men of good pleasure" and "good pleasure in men," would arrest the attention and prevent mistake from carelessness. If the change was intentional, the scribe could have best justified it by claiming that the accompanying construction was unchanged, while a probably original conformity to the case of εἰρήνη was restored. Is it not a sound textual principle that in variations the least possible disturbance of context is to be assumed?

(*c*) A song like this, short, easily remembered, and of intense interest to the Christian communities, must have been communicated largely by oral tradition. This makes for the same combination, whether the nominative or genitive were used. The phrase-meaning would naturally remain unchanged, while the variation in the last word would simply determine the relation of the phrase to εἰρήνη. The difference in meaning would pass for nothing in repetition from memory. The thought in both cases would be "peace on earth, good pleasure in men," the second phrase being in the one case an explanatory appositive, and in the other an explanatory genitive suggesting the origin of the peace.

This unstudied oral transmission, which leads us back of the scribe bending laboriously, or, as the case may be, carelessly, over his parchment, may be assumed from the very early difference between Luke and the Psalter. Indeed we do not know that Luke was the first to pen the angel-song in Greek. When therefore we find in the Codex Alexandrinus εὐδοκίας in Luke, and εὐδοκία in the Psalter, both from the hand of the same scribe, we may well suppose that both words came down independently from the time of those traditions spoken of by Luke in his Preface. It does not take many generations of manuscripts to reach from the fifth century to the first.

(*d*) If the order of words is an objection to combining εὐδοκία (nom.) with ἐν ἀνθρώποις—though we cannot but think it of small account—the objection is removed by the use of εὐδοκίας (gen.); for if εὐδοκίας, as modified by ἐν ἀνθρώποις, is combined with εἰρήνη, it would be a natural order even in prose to put ἐν ἀνθρώποις between the two. Without doubt, we should in prose look for the article after εἰρήνη—ἡ τῆς ἐν ἀνθρώποις εὐδοκίας—but this burst of song is not prose. No article is found in it, although the generosity of Greek might have given us six or seven in prose. Compare Luke xix. 38, ἐν οὐρανῷ εἰρήνη καὶ δόξα ἐν ὑψίστοις, where we might have had four articles.

This exegesis of Luke, reasonable when taken by itself, is thus strongly supported by the Psalter, in which the meaning "good pleasure in men" is, I cannot but think, the only one admissible. The case is not, indeed, the same as if another evangelist had given the reading εὐδοκία, but if Matthew had recorded the angel's song, and had written εὐδοκία, one could hardly avoid saying that both he and Luke were substantially at one, and meant "good pleasure in men."

Our general conclusion, then, is that the meaning of the second clause in Luke ii. 14 is "On earth peace—the peace of good pleasure in men," reconciliation with men, good-will towards men. It is a pleasant result of this discussion to find that what we still sing in the Gloria in Excelsis and what we read in the Greek of Luke are so closely alike. The peace on earth is "the peace of God," and the song of the heavenly host is constantly echoed in the gospel benedictions—"Grace, Mercy, and Peace."

II

’Ἐπιούσιος, TRANSLATED IN THE LORD'S PRAYER "DAILY."

Τὸν ἄρτον ἡμῶν τὸν ἐπιούσιον δὸς ἡμῖν σήμερον.
—Matt. vi. 11.
Τὸν ἄρτον ἡμῶν τὸν ἐπιούσιον δίδου ἡμῖν τὸ καθ' ἡμέραν.
—Luke xi. 3.

THE word ἐπιούσιος seems never to have been fully incorporated into the Greek language. Not found earlier than the New Testament, it has, even in later ecclesiastical Greek, the position of a quoted rather than an adopted word. In the New Testament itself it is found but twice, and practically but once.

§ 1. SKETCH OF THE HISTORY OF THE DISCUSSION.

’Ἐπιούσιος has undoubtedly received more lexical discussion than any other word in the New Testament. The long series goes back more than sixteen centuries, to the Father of Biblical Criticism. Origen in his "Treatise on Prayer," which is largely an exposition of the Lord's Prayer, says: "Since some suppose that we are told to pray for bread for the body, it is worth while, after having in this way refuted their false notions, to settle the truth in regard to the substantial (ἐπιούσιον) bread. . . . First, this must be understood, that the word ἐπιούσιον is found in none of the Greeks, being used neither by philosophers nor in the current speech of ordinary men, but it seems to have been formed by the Evangelists. At any rate Matthew and Luke agreed about the word, having brought it out without any difference whatever. The translators of the Hebrew have done the same in the case of other words. For who of the Greeks ever used the expression ἐνωτίζου [in-ear] or ἀκουτίσθητι [make-hear] instead of εἰς τὰ ὦτα δέξαι [receive into your ears] and ἀκοῦσαι ποιεῖς [cause you to hear]? Quite like ἐπιούσιος is a word in the writings of Moses, spoken by God, 'Ye shall be to me a people περιούσιος'; and both words seem to me to have been formed from οὐσία [substance]; the former meaning bread converted into our substance, the latter signifying a people employed about substance [what is substantial?] and devoted to it. . . . Just as bodily bread by being brought into union with the body for its nourishment passes into its substance, so the living bread that came down from heaven, being brought into union with the mind and the soul, imparts of its virtue to him who has given himself up to be nourished by it. And so will it be what we ask for as substantial bread."* Many points of remark are suggested by this, but I will speak only of etymology. The derivation given by Origen, which, whether original with him or not, has its earliest record in his writings, has had a long and honorable life, and finds an able advocacy, though with a different meaning, in one of the latest New Testament lexicons, the "Biblico-Theological Lexicon" of Prof. Hermann Cremer. In regard to the coining of the word by the Evangelists, Origen was, no doubt, influenced by his belief

---
*Orig. Op. Omn. I. Col. 505-511. (Migne Patr. Gr. XI.)

that Matthew first wrote in Hebrew, and then translated. A translator is more likely to coin words than an independent narrator. But if Matthew's Greek is the original, as most scholars now think, there may have been also a current Lord's Prayer in Greek, which was incorporated by both Matthew and Luke into their Gospels. Again, the word περιούσιος might deceive even Origen by a false analogy. We know that the philology of the ancients cannot be trusted, though it is not so with their usage. Ludicrous examples of false derivation can be found in Cicero, but perhaps only one case of error in the use of a word; and that we should hesitate to believe if he had not himself confessed it. It seems to me that the strongest point in favor of Origen's derivation—not explanation—of ἐπιούσιος is that he makes no account of the retention of the final letter of ἐπὶ in composition with οὐσία. This was a matter not of reasoning, but of Greek feeling. Was it simple inadvertence?

We ought next to notice the opinion of "the Latin Origen." Portions of Jerome's comment on Matt. vi. 11 are often quoted. Entire, it is as follows:—" What we have translated *super-substantialem* is given in Greek ἐπιούσιον, which word the Seventy Translators most frequently give as περιούσιον. We have examined therefore the Hebrew, and wherever they have used περιούσιον we have found SGOLIA,* which Symmachus has translated ἐξαίρετον, that is, pre-eminent or distinguished, although in a certain passage he has expressed it by

---
* סְגֻלָּה, Ex. xix. 5; Deut. vii. 6; xiv. 2; xxvi. 18.

peculiare [private treasure]. When, therefore, we ask of God to bestow upon us that bread which is a peculiar treasure, or pre-eminent, we ask for Him who says, 'I am the living bread, which came down from heaven.' In the Gospel which is called 'according to the Hebrews,' instead of supersubstantial bread I have found MAHAR, which means 'for to-morrow'; so that the sense is: Our bread for to-morrow, that is, for the future give us to-day. We can understand supersubstantial bread, also, in another way, as that which is above all substances and surpasses the whole world of creatures. Others suppose simply that the saints have a care for present food only, according to the language of the apostle who says, 'Having food and raiment, let us with these be content.' Accordingly, among the subsequent precepts is this one, 'Do not take thought for the morrow.' "*

Jerome here presents four meanings of ἐπιούσιος, his own preference being the first. His identifying περιούσιος and ἐπιούσιος is rather surprising from a philological point of view, but he evidently looks at the matter practically, and follows his master Origen in ascribing about the same meaning to both. The fourth meaning, "present bread," comes from giving to ἔπειμι the sense of πάρειμι. But the point of chief interest is the reference to the "Gospel according to the Hebrews," which means not simply a Gospel written in Hebrew, but a Gospel composed, or received, by certain Hebrews. In Book III.

---

*Hieron. op. omn. vii. Col. 44. (Migne, Patrol. Lat. Vol. 26.) In Evan. Matt. Lib. I. Cap. vi.

Contra Pelagium he describes it as the gospel written in the Chaldaic and Syrian language in Hebrew letters, and used even to his day by the Nazarenes.* He also, on Matt. xii. 13, speaks of "the Gospel which the Nazarenes and Ebionites use, which lately we translated from Hebrew into Greek, and which is called by most the original Gospel of Matthew."†

He also states that he has translated it into Latin and that Origen often makes use of it.‡

This reference to the Hebrew, or Aramaic, Gospel is a testimony, whatever it may be worth, to the derivation from ἐπί and ἰέναι. If it were the original of Matthew, it would also settle the meaning of the word. But if it was simply a translation, like its Syriac sisters, or an Ebionitic tractate, then its MAHAR is merely the opinion of an unknown author of an almost unknown version.§ This leads to the question, Why did not Jerome, and why also did not Origen follow the rendering of ἐπιούσιος found in the Hebrew Gospel? And the only possible answer is that neither of them believed this Gospel to be the original of Matthew, or otherwise authoritative.

---

*In Evangelio juxta Hebraeos, quod Chaldaico quidem Syroque sermone, sed Hebraicis litteris, scriptum est, quo utuntur usque hodie Nazareni. Migne's edition II 785.

†In Evangelio, quo utuntur Nazaraeni et Ebionitae (quod nuper in Graecum de Hebraeo sermone transtulimus, et quod vocatur a plerisque Matthaei authenticum). Migne vii. 77.

‡Evangelium quoque quod appellatur secundum Hebraeos, et a me nuper in Graecum Latinumque sermonem translatum est, quo et Origines saepe utitur. Migne ii. 831.

§All the extant fragments of this Gospel may be found in Hilgenfeld's "Novum Testamentum extra Canonem," Fasc. iv. Ed. ii p. 15. They contain but twenty-five Hebrew words, and with all the Greek and Latin interpretations occupy but two and a half pages. There is a thoroughly annotated edition by E. B. Nicholson, Bodleian Librarian, London, 1879.

It is a long step—in time and in style—from Jerome to Calvin, and to the following pithy lines: "Because the kindness of God flows in a continuous course for our nourishment, the bread that he supplies is called ἐπιούσιος, that is, *superveniens* [still-coming], for so we may render it; as much as to say: Lord, since daily our life has need of new nourishments, be thou never wearied in constantly bestowing them."*

If the great theologian had had as much influence in this exegesis as in his theology, a world of subsequent discussion would have been saved. The meaning of "superveniens" may be illustrated from Horace, where he says, speaking of the transitoriness of our possessions,—

Sic quia perpetuus nulli datur usus, et heres
Heredem alterius velut unda *supervenit* undam.
Ep. ii. 2, 175-6.

Calvin's implied etymology shows that the derivation from ἐπιέναι, which he does not think it necessary to discuss, was familiar to scholars.

In passing from Calvin to Tholuck one omits between fifty and sixty of the seventy-five "philologians and theologians" mentioned by the latter in his discussion of this word. This discussion is found in the "Exposition of the Sermon on the Mount," pages 341-353 of the edition in English.† It is marked by great learning and acute-

---

*Quia Dei benignitas continuo tenore ad nos pascendos fluit, panis quem ministrat vocatur ἐπιούσιος, hoc est, superveniens: sic enim interpretari licet. Tantundem ergo volet hoc nomen acsi dictum esset: Domine, quum quotidie novis alimentis opus habeat vita nostra, ne assidue ea largiendo unquam fatigeris.—Ioannis Calvini in Harmoniam ex Matthaeo, Marco et Luca compositam Commentarii. Berolini, 1833. Ed. Tholuck, Vol. i. p. 169.

†Brown's translation (T. & T. Clark, Edinburgh, 1860), which is from the fourth German edition, 1856. The first German edition was published in 1833.

ness, and especially by the great number of quoted opinions. That the author does not refer to Calvin is the more noticeable because he himself edited the Commentary from which I have quoted.

He opens by saying, "This word has been the subject of numerous learned disquisitions, yet is there room for new investigations. Scultetus calls the interpretation of ἐπιούσιος *carnificina theologorum et grammaticorum.*"

The derivation of the word is fully considered, with this conclusion: "Great as are the difficulties in the way of deriving ἐπιούσιος from εἶναι, yet, even were they greater, we must still give the preference to that derivation, and for this reason, that it is impossible, on the supposition of its derivation from ἐπιοῦσα, to find in it any meaning in keeping with the context." (P. 346.) "The notion of Ernesti that the prayer was to be offered in the *evening*, so that then one would literally pray to-day for the bread of to-morrow, looks like jesting." (P. 345.)

The meaning is given thus: "The ἐπιούσιον is something between τὸ ἐλλιπές and the περιττόν or the περιούσιον, and denotes that which is just enough. So understood, the prayer has many analogies in the Old and New Testaments; compare, for example, Prov. xxx. 8, where Solomon prays, "Keep far from me poverty and riches."" (P. 348.)

The discussion closes with a refutation of the mystical view that ἐπιούσιος refers to spiritual bread. The whole discussion is a noble exemplification of modern Biblical scholarship.

The next specially noteworthy discussion of ἐπιούσιος is the contribution of philological scholarship. Leo Meyer devotes to it twenty-nine pages in the "Zeitschrift für vergleichende Sprachforschung," Vol. vii., pp. 401-430. (Berlin, 1858.) Herodotus, Xenophon, Plato, Demosthenes and the tragedians are brought into the field as well as the Biblical writers, and one page contains forty references to Homer on the question of ἐπί with or without its final vowel. The two etymologies—from εἶναι and ἰέναι—are considered at length, and comparative etymology is not neglected. It is only after more than twenty pages of historical and philological preparation that we reach the announcement, "Wir kommen nun zu ἐπιούσιος selbst." He derives it from ἐπί and ὀντ-, and gives the principal meaning to the preposition. Ἐπιούσιος "is being for something," i. e., useful, serviceable. While the linguistic value of this essay is great, the artificial aspect of the proposed word-building makes it seem more like a philological specimen than an actual word. Ancient versions are not discussed, except that a page is given to the Gothic. This is valuable, as would be expected from the author's scholarship in that field.

This short sketch—mere fragments of an outline—of the lexical history of ἐπιούσιος began with the greatest of the Fathers, and may fitly end with one of the greatest of modern Patristic scholars. When the revisers were at the beginning of their work, Bishop Lightfoot, certainly their leader, issued (1871) his book "On a Fresh

Revision of the English New Testament," with an appendix on the words ἐπιούσιος, περιούσιος. This is Appendix I. of the third edition (1891), which I use. To ἐπιούσιος forty-three pages are given (217-260). The divisions are (1) The etymology of the word, (2) The requirements of the sense, (3) The tenor of tradition. All but seven pages is devoted to the third division. Of this he says (p. 219): "It was chiefly the conviction that justice had not been done to its consideration which led me to institute the investigation afresh." Under the third division he discusses the derivation of the word as found (1) in the Greek Fathers, (2) in the Aramaic versions, especially the Curetonian Syriac, and the Gospel according to the Hebrews, (3) in the Egyptian versions, and (4) in the Latin,—especially the Old Latin. The two lines given to the Gothic (p. 258) can be supplemented by the page of Leo Meyer already referred to. Earliest tradition is shown to favor the derivation from ἐπιέναι.

§ 2. ETYMOLOGY AND MEANING.

In regard to the etymology, we might make short work of it, so far as Greek is concerned, if we could adopt the desperate conjecture of Dr. Cureton, who thinks that ἐπιούσιος was formed from the Aramaic by transliteration.* Letting this pass, we have first to choose between the derivation from ἐπί and εἶναι, or οὐσία, and ἐπί and ἰέναι. I assume the latter, referring the reader to Lightfoot and Thayer's Lexicon for the reasons. But the der-

---
*See preface to his edition of the Curetonian Syriac Version, "Remains of a very Antient Recension," etc., p. xviii.

ivation from ἐπιέναι may be on either of two lines: (1) from ἐπιοῦσα, with ἡμέρα supplied, or (2) from the participle ἐπιών direct. The former yields a somewhat different meaning from the latter, and is adopted by the best authorities. Winer says (N. T. Grammar, p. 97, Thayer's ed.): " Ἐπιούσιος has probably direct relation to the fem. (ἡ) ἐπιοῦσα, sc. ἡμέρα, and accordingly ἄρτος ἐπιούσιος means 'bread for the following day.'" To this two objections are made which certainly are worth considering.

1. The first has reference to its form. The adjective formed by -ιος from ἐπιοῦσα, as a substantive, would regularly be ἐπιουσαῖος, like δευτεραῖος (Acts xxviii. 13), τεταρταῖος (John xi. 39), δεκαταῖος, etc. This objection seems to have originated with Salmasius. Bishop Lightfoot questions the validity of it on two grounds: "The termination -αῖος in all these adjectives is suggested by the long -α or -η of the primitives from which they are derived, δευτέρα, τρίτη, etc.; and the short ending of ἐπιοῦσα is not a parallel case. Moreover, the meaning is not the same; for the adjectives in -αῖος fix a date, *e. g.* τεταρταῖος ἦλθεν, 'he came on the fourth day,' whereas the sense which we require here is much more general, implying simply *possession* or connection."*

One may be pardoned for expressing some surprise at this paragraph, for (1) What evidence have we that the quantity of the nominative ending was regarded? These adjectives are formed on the original ā stem, as their

---
*On a Fresh Revision of the English New Testament, Appendix i.

deviation from η shows. The stem-ending was long in all first-declension feminines, and always so appeared in the genitive and dative cases, whatever the quantity of the nominative. I have here and there lighted on the following examples of adjectives in -αῖος from short-ending feminines of this declension: ἀρουραῖος, ἀελλαῖος, ἁμαξαῖος, ἐχιδναῖος, θαλασσαῖος, μελισσαῖος, μοιραῖος, Πισαῖος, χαλαζαῖος, Æolic Μοισαῖος. True, we have adjectives in -ιος from nouns of short endings, as δίψιος, and not διψαῖος, from δίψα; but we also have those in -ιος from nouns of long endings, as τίμιος, ἑσπέριος, ἡμέριος, and never τιμαῖος, etc. Without doubt, there are more adjectives in -αῖος from long-vowel nouns than from short, but I suppose there are a great many more feminine substantives ending in -η and -ā than in -ă. Further, while the final stem-vowel is long in the primaries, it is *shortened* in forming the diphthong αι. Otherwise the ending would be -ᾳος. How, then, is -αῖος even "suggested" more by a long nominative ending than by a short one? (2) These numerical adjectives are not confined to the fixing of dates, as the lexicons abundantly show. Their suffix -ιος is general and indefinite. When they agree with the subject of a verb, as commonly, the date-force is inferential. Τεταρταῖος ἦλθεν is literally "a fourth-day man he came." Ἄρτος τεταρταῖος would mean "bread of the fourth day," and ἄρτος ἐπιουσαῖος "bread of the next day." For the very reason that they all imply ἡμέρα in their primaries, they would attract a newcomer, like ἐπιουσαῖος, to their form. This objection, then, whatever may be its value, seems to be well sustained.

2. The second objection has been made to rest on the incongruity introduced, and which can be seen by reading the two passages thus: "Give us this day our bread for the morrow," "Give us day by day our bread for the morrow." As I have felt this objection strongly myself, I perhaps have the right now to say that it has been greatly over-rated, for ἡ ἐπιοῦσα ἡμέρα is not precisely equivalent to ἡ αὔριον. Lightfoot shows plainly enough (p. 226) the difference, and illustrates it by referring to the Ecclesiazusae of Aristophanes, lines 20, 105, to which might be added 83-85. A much better illustration is furnished by A. H. Wratislaw in his pamphlet entitled "New evidence as to the origin and meaning of ἐπιούσιος in the Lord's Prayer." Plato's "Crito" opens with the question of Socrates as to why Crito comes so early to the prison. It is early dawn (ὄρθρος βαθύς). He is the bearer of sad news; the ship from Delos will be here to-day (τήμερον), and therefore Socrates must die to-morrow (εἰσαύριον). Socrates does not believe that the ship will arrive to-day (τήμερον). He promises to give his reason, and then repeats his statement in this form: Οὐ τοίνυν τῆς ἐπιούσης ἡμέρας οἶμαι αὐτὸ ἥξειν, ἀλλὰ τῆς ἑτέρας. It cannot be doubted that τήμερον and ἐπιούσης refer to the same day. Other examples introduced by Mr. Wratislaw do not seem to me correctly explained, but this one is clear and sufficient. It may be paralleled from the Book of Common Prayer, which, in Morning Prayer for families,

speaks of being "brought in safety to the beginning of *this day*," and further on implores "grace and protection for the *ensuing day*."

There is no absurdity, then, in saying, "Give us this day our bread for the coming day;" but, at the same time, every one must feel the scant need of the addition, "for the coming day." The petition comes unpleasantly near tautology, and that too without emphasis. The same impression is made by the language of Luke, "Give us day by day our bread for the coming day," but with less propriety in the connection.

If, now, we put this impression of tautology beside the serious objection to the form, already considered, there is reason enough for examining carefully the other derivation from ἐπιέναι, viz., from ἐπιών, disconnected from the notion of "day," especially as the Old Syriac version suggests a meaning that could arise in no other way. Such a derivation is countenanced by the words ἐθέλων ἐθελούσιος, ἑκών ἑκούσιος. This last pair we find in the New Testament (1 Cor. ix. 17; Philemon, 14). Lightfoot, indeed, remarks (p. 223), "No motive existed for introducing an adjective by the side of ἐπιών, sufficiently powerful to produce the result in an advanced stage of the language, when the fertility of creating new forms had been greatly impaired." But such *a priori* decisions must be received with great caution. And do not new forms abound in the later times of a language, when word-making becomes more conscious, as the language itself is more the object of study, and writers try to escape the monotony of a fixed vocabulary? At any rate, the New Testament, though a small volume, contains nearly nine hundred words not found in Greek literature before (and including) Aristotle. Most of these bear obvious marks of derivation, showing themselves to be comparatively recent, and not old popular words lifted into literary use.

The existence of the participle, then, does not forbid the existence of the similar adjective. The adjective turns the single act into a general or habitual state. Ἐθέλων means "wishing," ἐθελούσιος "voluntary." The ending -ιος is like the English -*y*. Compare "snowing" and "snowy." Ὁ ἐπιὼν ἄρτος, literally "the on-coming bread," might mean the next loaf that should come on the table, but ὁ ἐπιούσιος ἄρτος would mean, not the *next*, but, if we had such a word, "*next-y* bread," i. e., bread that we expect continuously, continually, the constant supply of bread; in colloquial parlance, "bread right along." If the point be pressed that ἐπιούσιος is a very unusual word, and unlikely to arise in the way now supposed, the answer is that it comes from a very common participle by means of a suffix that is very common. The participle is so common that it is even used substantively, ἡμέρα being understood, for "the next day," ἐπιοῦσα. To illustrate again from English, if one should coin the word "*freez-y*," it might seem strange, and might never be adopted into the language, but it would be perfectly intelligible, so long as we say " freez-ing."

In regard to form, the stem ἐπιοντ- would by regular

euphonic changes become ἐπιους-, very nearly as its feminine becomes ἐπιοῦσα.

One cannot be quite satisfied with any explanation of this word that does not suggest some Hebrew equivalent or Aramaic original. Now, if it contains the notion of a constant supply of need, a continuous bestowment, then we naturally look for some Hebrew expression for continual, perhaps daily, work and service At once we think of the "continual" offerings and the daily services of the sanctuary. The "continual burnt-offering" which was to be offered "day by day" (Ex. xxix. 38, 42) was עֹלַת תָּמִיד, "offering of continuance." In the same use of תָּמִיד we find "men of continuance" (Ezek. xxxix. 14), i. e., men employed in regular, constant work; "diet of continuance," given to Jehoiachin "every day" (Jer. lii. 34), and even "bread of continuance" (Num. iv. 7), applied to the shew-bread. So much was תָּמִיד used in association with the daily burnt-offering that in later usage it stands alone for the offering itself. In Dan. viii. 11, 12, 13; xi. 31; xii. 11, it is, literally, the "continuance" that is "taken away." Our common version has it, the "daily sacrifice"; the Revision more accurately, the "continual burnt-offering."

תָּמִיד is usually translated in the Septuagint by διαπαντός, as, οἱ ἄρτοι οἱ διαπαντός, Num. iv. 7; several times, mostly in later usage, by ἐνδελεχισμός, as θυσίαν ἐνδελεχισμοῦ, Ex. xxix. 42; ὁλοκαυτώσεις ἐνδελεχισμοῦ, 2 Esdr. iii. 5. The most remarkable translation is in Num. iv. 16, ἡ θυσία ἡ καθ' ἡμέραν, which seems to be the begin-

ning of that confusion of meanings—continual, daily—
amounting to a side-development, that has come down to
our day. It is noticeable that no adjective is used in these
renderings. Whether ἐπιούσιος would have been sometimes used, if in existence, we need not inquire. The
usual phrase in the Vulgate is *juge sacrificium*—this
adjective being used by Horace to describe a perennial
fountain, *jugis aquæ fons* (Sat. ii. 6, 2).

§ 3. THREE EARLY VERSIONS.

The meaning "constant, continual," which is, to say
the least, illustrated by the Hebrew, seems to be confirmed
by the three most important ancient versions, Old
Syriac, Old Latin, and Gothic. To begin with the
latest—about A. D. 350—in the Gothic version Matt. vi.
11 (the corresponding passage in Luke is lost) reads:
Hlaif unsarana thana sinteinan gif uns himma daga;
which may be Englished, with no regard to the Greek,
word for word: "Bread ours the continual give us
this day." *Sinteinan* (nom. *sinteins*) is given in all the
glossaries as "daily." Massman, however, and Bernhardt
(1884) give two meanings, "immerwährend, täglich." Leo
Meyer in his "Gothische Sprache" (p. 98 *et al.*) gives
"fortwährend, täglich." Kluge, under *Sündflut*, gives
"täglich, immerwährend" and compares the plant-name
sin-grün, the Anglo-Saxon *sin-grene* and *symle*, and
the Latin *semper*. The same prefix is seen at least
twice in Béowulf—*sin-gal*, "continual" (154), and *sin-
niht*, "night after night" (161). No one would ques-

tion its connection with *sinteino*, a common adverb meaning "always." This is found in Mark v. 5 for the original διαπαντός, in xiv. 7 for πάντοτε, in xv. 8 for ἀεί. The origin of the last part of the word is not perfectly clear. Kluge would take it as an obsolete root meaning "day" (see Ety. Dict. under "Tag"), and gives "täglich" as the first meaning. Certainly, the notion of "day" lapsed, and "continual," as the adverb shows, was the regular meaning. Probably the chief reason for making *sinteins* mean "daily," is that *seiteins*, a collateral form, is used in 2 Cor. xi. 28 for ἡ καθ' ἡμέραν, where Paul speaks of "that which presseth upon me *daily*, anxiety for all the churches." But here *sinteins* might have its proper meaning of "continual" without wandering far from the Greek original. Whether, however, "daily" or "continual" is the primary meaning, the difference is not essential as to its representation of ἐπιούσιος. It does not mean "for the coming day," but "constantly recurring."

Let us next consider the Old Latin version, or bundle of versions. Here we find in Matthew "Panem nostrum cotidianum da nobis hodie"; and in Luke "Panem nostrum cotidianum da nobis cotidie."* Whence came this "cotidianum"? Certainly not from a literal translation of ἐπιούσιος, considered by itself. If the Evangelists had wanted a Greek word to express "daily," there was one ready to hand, found in the writers of that time, and even

---

*Old Latin Biblical Texts; No III. The Four Gospels. By Henry J. White. Clarendon Press, 1888. Codex *Monacensis* (q). Some codices—I do not know how many—have in Luke the error of "hodie" instead of "cotidie." The received Vulgate text has also "hodie" in Luke, but the best text, Codex Amiatinus, has "cotidie."

in the New Testament. James comes very near ἄρτος ἐφήμερος when he says (ii. 15), "If a brother or sister be naked and in lack of daily food"— τῆς ἐφημέρου τροφῆς. The Latin Vulgate for this is, of course, "victu quotidiano." In the absence of any such original in the Lord's Prayer, it is possible to account for the "cotidianum" either by the influence of the context—the σήμερον of Matthew, and particularly the καθ' ἡμέραν of Luke, serving to attract and specialize the general idea of "continual"—or by a larger association with continual worship through daily offerings, or in a more general way by the tendency to speak of the ordinary, constant things of life as "daily." It can hardly be that "cotidianum" came from ἐπιούσιον in the sense of "for the morrow"; for the legitimate development of *crastinus* would be to *futurus*, as Jerome says, on this very passage, "*crastinum, id est futurum.*" So the Hebrew מָחָר means "in time to come" in Deut. vi. 20 and in other passages.*

---

*This "cotidianum" must be the parent of the "daily" of modern versions—a rendering that will probably hold its own in spite of grammars, dictionaries and commentaries. Jerome's version has "supersubstantialem" in Matthew, and it is hard to believe that he did not put the same word in Luke. If so, then "cotidianum" was forced into the text of Luke by the pressure of the Old Latin. Westcott and Hort say (N. T. II. 81)—with no reference to this word—"Scribes accustomed to older forms of text corrupted by unwitting reminiscence the Vulgate which they were copying; so that an appreciable part of Jerome's work had been imperceptibly undone when the Vulgate attained its final triumph." The wonder is that Matthew was left unchanged, which was due perhaps to the support of Jerome's Commentary.

' Supersubstantialem" has left its long mark on some modern Roman Catholic versions. The Rheims version (1582), which is the basis of the present English Catholic Bible, reads, "Give us this day our supersubstantial bread." The edition that I have—an American edition with archiepiscopal sanction—has this foot-note: "In St. Luke the same word is rendered 'daily bread.' It is understood of the bread of life which we receive in the Blessed Sacrament." Wyclif, who translated from the Latin Vulgate, gives "ouir other substance." The Dutch version (Antwerp, 1598) has "overweselyck," like the "ofer-wistlic" of the ancient Northumbrian interlinear Gospel (Lindisfarne MS.) On the other hand, in spite of the authority of the Vulgate, all the French versions have "notre pain quotidien," the authorized Italian has "Il pane nostro

By far the most important versional testimony to the meaning of ἐπιούσιος comes from the Old Syriac Gospels. The Curetonian fragments, published in 1858, and the Sinai MS., published in 1894,—the latter containing only the first petition of the Prayer in Matthew—agree in having for ἐπιούσιος ܐܡܝܢܐ (in the old characters ܐܡܝܢܐ, in Hebrew characters אָמִינָא, in English, with continental vowel-sounds, *amīna*, to be compared with our *amen* from Hebrew). The meaning of the Syriac word is sufficiently attested by its biblical usage. In the New Testament it is used once, adverbially, to translate διαπαντός, "*always* a conscience void of offence" (Acts xxiv. 16); several times for προσκαρτερέω, "*continued steadfastly*" (Acts ii. 46); also for πυκνός, "thine *often* infirmities" (1 Tim. v. 23); for προσμένω, "*continueth* in supplications" (1 Tim. v. 5); for ἐκτενῶς, "prayer was made *without ceasing*" [Rev. earnestly], (Acts xii. 5); for ἀδιάλειπτος, "remembering *without ceasing*" (1 Thess. i. 3). These examples, being outside of the Gospels, are from the Peshitto version.

In the Old Testament, where the word is of frequent occurrence, it regularly represents, often adverbially, the Hebrew תָּמִיד. It is found in every part of the Old Testament, except the Psalms. Thus Aaron's breast-

---

quotidiano," and the German, "Gib uns heute unser tägliches Brod." This is taken from the translation of Dr. Allioli, "the only authorized German version duly approved by the Apostolic See." To it is appended the following note, which, it will be observed, is not an exposition of the Vulgate, but of the Greek:—"Wörtlich, unser zur Wesenheit (Nothdurft) gehöriges Brod, diess ist das Tägliche. Darunter ist alles verstanden was zum Unterhalte der Seele und des Leibes nothwendig ist,—das göttliche Wort, der Leib des Herrn, die tägliche nothdürftige Nahrung. (Chrys. Theophl. Aug. Cypr.)." This last is substantially translated from the Glossa Ordinaria—"panis Corpus Christi est, ut verbum Dei, vel ipse Deus, quo quotidie egemus," cited by Tholuck on Matt. vi. 2.

plate is a memorial "*continually*" (Ex. xxviii. 29). The burnt offering is "*continual*" (xxix. 42). The fire is to be "*ever*" on the altar (Lev. vi. 13). The shew-bread is "*continual*" (Num. iv. 7). Nine times in the twenty-ninth chapter of Numbers the word is applied to the "daily burnt offering." The eyes of the Lord are "*always*" upon the land of promise (Deut. xi. 12). Elisha passeth by "*continually*" (2 Kings iv. 9). The trumpets sound "*continually*" before the ark (1 Chron. xvi. 6). And so on in Ezra, Nehemiah, Proverbs, Isaiah ("*continually* upon the watch tower," xxi. 8), Jeremiah, Ezekiel ("men of *continual* employment," xxxix. 14), Daniel (Hebrew portions), and elsewhere. I have verified more than sixty examples in which ܐܡܝܢܐ translates תָּמִיד. The Syriac word, then, according to biblical usage, means continual, constant. The dictionaries, covering a wider than biblical usage, give the meanings, *stabilis, constans, assiduus, perpetuus*. The meaning, then, of the whole phrase would be, "Our constant supply of bread."

Now, what is the value of this rendering as to the meaning of ἐπιούσιος? Dr. Chase in his "Lord's Prayer in the Early Church"* says: "It is difficult to see that it represents any probable meaning of ἐπιούσιος." Carrying out a suggestion of Dr. Cureton, he thinks that the Greek word, not being understood by the translator, was represented "by a classical phrase about bread in the Old Testament, slightly changed." Now it is true that

---
*Texts and Studies. Vol. I., No. 3, The Lord's Prayer in the Early Church. By Frederic Henry Chase, B. D. Cambridge, 1891, pp. 42-53.

among the great variety of actions to which the Syriac word is applied in the Old Testament, it is two or three times applied to eating bread. Mephibosheth is to "eat bread *continually* at David's table" (2 Sam. ix. 7, 10), and Jehoiachin "did eat bread *continually*" with the king of Babylon (2 Kings xxv. 29; Jer. lii. 33). These, so far as I can discover, are the only cases of association with ordinary bread. Twice, also adverbially, it is used of the shew-bread (Num. iv. 7; 2 Chron. ii. 4), but I can find no example of its use as a *descriptive epithet* of bread. Even if we assume, perhaps ungraciously, that the translator was in serious doubt, it is hard to see how his mind would be influenced much by any "classical phrase about bread in the Old Testament."

Dr. Chase's position is that ἐπιούσιος, coming as it does from ἡ ἐπιοῦσα, introduces tautology into the prayer, and is "alien to its simplicity of language." It probably, then, does not belong to the earliest prayer, but is "due to liturgical use." The original clause, "Our bread of the day give to us," was changed to "our bread for the coming day," to adapt the prayer to use at evening. This "working hypothesis" is presented with a modest ingenuity that almost fascinates one; but it seems to me that if we restore to ἐπιούσιος the meaning found in the Old Syriac, the hypothesis is no longer needed. The tautology complained of arises from deriving ἐπιούσιος directly from ἡ ἐπιοῦσα. All other tautology is due to translation, the disabilities of which ought not to be charged to the original. "Day by day our daily" is tautological, in a narrow sense, but "day by day our constant supply" is not, in any sense. Nor does the hypothesis seem to be securely based on liturgical need. If I should venture to mark out a liturgical development of the clause, I should by no means omit from the primary the idea of constant supply contained in ἐπιούσιος. To this might very naturally be added σήμερον for morning prayer, and the more general τὸ καθ' ἡμέραν for other occasions. If, however, ἐπιούσιος means "of the coming day," and that means "of the present day," why should σήμερον ever have been added? Dr. Chase's answer is, "There meets us a double rendering of the original word" (p. 47). But if we give to ἐπιούσιος the Old Syriac meaning, there is no room for the tautology of a "double rendering," and no need of reconstructing the clause as we now find it, further than to acknowledge the varying traditions of σήμερον and τὸ καθ' ἡμέραν. Further, the coining of a new word, which ἐπιούσιος is acknowledged to be, seems likely to arise from a more pressing need than liturgical convenience, as, for example, from the demand of a Semitic original. The absence of any word for ἐπιούσιος in a reference to the Prayer by Ephrem Syrus is urged by Dr. Chase (p. 50) in favor of a form of the petition earlier than that of the Gospels; but an incidental reference in a sermon, and the omission of a seemingly unessential word, is surely small evidence that he was quoting from an earlier and superior authority. Still more inconclusive is the evidence from Tatian. The rendering adopted by Chase, "Give us the bread of our day," is not sustained by Hill's Diatessaron, which reads (p. 79), "Give us the sustenance [lit. power] of to-day." Dr. Charles Taylor in the Guardian (Jan. 6, 1897) renders, "Give us the necessity of the day;" which is practically the same as Murdock's Peshitto, "Our needful bread." Instead of omitting ἐπιούσιος, Tatian omits "bread," and emphasizes ἐπιούσιος, according to the meaning of the Peshitto.

In regard to the value of this testimony I would say:

1. The rendering is simple and clear, and betrays no wavering and no effort to solve an etymological difficulty. In this last respect it is in contrast with the Peshitto rendering, which means "bread of our necessity." This seems like an attempt to carry out a certain theory of the etymology of the Greek word, viz., that it is compounded of ἐπί and οὐσία, the latter meaning *essence*, that which is essential, then that which is necessary, or οὐσία meaning *existence*, as is advocated by Cremer in his Lexicon, and the compound adjective meaning "for, i. e., necessary for, existence." The Jerusalem Syriac rendering seems to have a similar origin—"bread of our abundance," οὐσία having the sense of *substance*, then wealth, abundance.* In contrast with all this, the Old Syriac gives a simple, intelligible word that has the appearance of be-

---

*I know nothing at first hand of this Jerusalem version, but am indebted for the rendering given above to the kindness of Dr. Isaac H. Hall. I cannot leave his name on this page without a few words of tribute to his worth, and of sorrow at his too early death. Our acquaintance began over the pages of Xenophon's Anabasis, when he was a boy in Norwalk, Conn. He needed little instruction in his textbook, for the spirit of the independent scholar was in him then. Of his achievements in Syriac scholarship I am not qualified to speak, but I can speak warmly of his generous heart and his willingness to place his learning at the service of others.

ing based on known usage, or on some ground other than philological reasoning.

2. The Old Syriac rendering connects, indirectly, ἐπιούσιος with the Hebrew תָּמִיד. If the Septuagint and later Greek versions had translated this Hebrew word by ἐπιούσιος, no one would ever have doubted the meaning of the latter, and a world of discussion would have been saved. No such translation is found, but we do find that this one Syriac version makes ἐπιούσιος the equivalent of a well known equivalent of תָּמִיד. So far as this goes, it serves to identify the rare Greek word with a very common Hebrew word.

3. The early date of the Old Syriac version ought to be taken into account. Bishop Westcott places it in the second century. The fact that we hear only of the Gospels in this version points to a very early origin. Is it, then, improbable that the version reaches back into the influence of tradition, and that the Syriac rendering gives us a traditional meaning?

4. We may, I think, go further, if we go carefully. I assume that the speech of the Jews in the time of Christ was bilingual—Aramaic, or early Jewish Syriac, and Greek. This matter is fully discussed by Professor Hadley in Smith's Dictionary of the Bible.* For our present purpose it is sufficient to take the case of Paul speaking to the Jews in Jerusalem, as described in Acts xxii. He at once gained the attention of his hearers by speaking in Aramaic ("Hebrew tongue"). They had evidently ex-

---

*Vol. ii., p. 1590, Am. Ed.

pected to hear him speak Greek. It seems that they would have understood him in either language, but the Aramaic pleased them. This may have been because the Aramaic was their national and domestic tongue, and they were more familiar with it. If this was true of the multitude in their chief city, it would be emphatically true of the dwellers in Galilee, and the country districts generally. It must be, therefore, that Jesus largely used the Aramaic in his teachings. The Lord's Prayer certainly was spoken by him in Aramaic, and may also have been spoken in Greek.

In regard to the bilingual character of this Prayer, two suppositions are possible. (1) Two forms of the Prayer may have existed side by side from the first. Then if ἐπιούσιος was in the Greek form, ܐܡܝܢܐ, or some modification of it, would very likely have been in the other; so that both words would come down together, and a very early Syriac translator of the Gospel would find his word supplied by tradition. (2) The other supposition is that the Prayer in Aramaic was strictly the original, but that the translation into Greek was made in Palestine, while both languages were familiar. Now a large part of the mystery of ἐπιούσιος, viz., its isolation in the language, will vanish, if we think of it as itself a translation. Translators are inclined to coin words, as the Septuagint abundantly testifies, many of the new words of which, but not all, lived to find place in the New Testament. But if the Greek word is a translation, what original is so probable as the one which afterwards, in meaning if not in form, appeared in the Old Syriac?

It is pleasant to think that the rendering "daily bread" is not far from the meaning of the Greek original, as interpreted by the early Syriac. It came to us, no doubt, from the Old Latin *cotidianum*, but this might come easily from the notion of continual. The affinity of "continual" and "daily" is well illustrated in the parallelism of the Received Version of Psalm lxxii. 15:

"Prayer also shall be made for him *continually*,
And *daily* [Rev. all the day long] shall he be praised."

With this may be fitly joined, from a modern Jewish Prayer-Book, the closing words of The Grace after Meals—"Thanks for the food wherewith thou dost feed and sustain us *continually* (the original is תָּמִיד) every day and hour."

III

DOES THE LORD'S PRAYER MAKE MENTION OF THE DEVIL?

'Ρῦσαι ἡμᾶς ἀπὸ τοῦ πονηροῦ.   Matt. vi. 13.

Is τοῦ πονηροῦ masculine or neuter; and does it mean the Evil One, or evil? The question is an exceedingly difficult one—more difficult than important—but the Revised Version has forced it upon us by its translation "Deliver us from the Evil One." The difficulty comes from the great mass of indecisive material that enters into the discussion. This may be seen from the debate that arose in England immediately after the publication of the Revised New Testament. The learned, and almost authoritative, defense of the Revision in the letters of Bishop Lightfoot are republished in Appendix II. of the third edition (1891) of his work "On a Fresh Revision of the New Testament." A more elaborate support of the same conclusion is found in "The Lord's Prayer in the Early Church" (Camb. Univ. Press, 1891), by Dr. Frederic H. Chase, who devotes more than half of his treatise to this word. The following points, among those ably argued in these treatises, must be classed, I think, as indecisive, though relevant.

1. The connection of thought. Probably few interpreters would go as far as Alford, on the one side, and

say, "The introduction of the mention of the evil one would here be quite incongruous and even absurd," and if an equally strong statement should be found on the other side we should have to ascribe both to personal bent rather than to definite exegetical principles. The idea of temptation goes well with the mention of the tempter, but equally well with the idea of that evil into which temptation may bring us. The word ῥῦσαι suggests rescue from a person, but is also used of deliverance from death (ὃς ἐκ τηλικούτου θανάτου ἐρύσατο ἡμᾶς, 2 Cor. i. 10), from the power of darkness (ὃς ἐρύσατο ἡμᾶς ἐκ τῆς ἐξουσίας τοῦ σκότους, Col. i. 13), and from every evil work (ῥύσεταί με ὁ Κύριος ἀπὸ παντὸς ἔργου πονηροῦ, 2 Tim. iv. 18).

2. The distinction between ἀπό and ἐκ. While ἐκ might suggest *things* rather than *persons*, and ἀπό the reverse, we find this distinction not sanctioned by usage. See the full and candid discussion of these prepositions by Chase (pp. 70-84).

3. The New Testament use of the concrete instead of the abstract. We may acknowledge, with Meyer, its general tone in this respect, without finding such a preponderance of the concrete as will have decisive weight in interpreting any single word. There are no philosophical abstracts in the New Testament, but moral abstracts are abundant. The term morality (ἠθική) is wanting, but all the elements of morality, all the moral virtues, are present in their usual phraseology. What is more to the point, we find the abstract used in cases where the concrete would be expected. Twice in the twelfth chapter

of Romans we read of good and evil where, if it were not for the unmistakable neuter article, we might think that persons were meant: Ἀπυστυγοῦντες τὸ πονηρόν, κολλώμενοι τῷ ἀγαθῷ (ver. 9). Is not the evil *person* whom we abhor, and the good person to whom we cleave? But the article silences our wise question. Again, after reading (ver. 20) of the personal enemy who hungers, and thirsts, and feels the coals of fire on his head, we find the thought broadening out into that grand generalization: Μὴ νικῶ ὑπὸ τοῦ κακοῦ, ἀλλὰ νίκα ἐν τῷ ἀγαθῷ τὸ κακόν (ver. 21).

One may say, This is Paul, not Matthew. Let us come back, then, to Matthew, and to the words of our Lord as recorded by him, and to the Sermon on the Mount. Dr. Chase says (p. 95), "The use of abstract terms seems alien to the spirit of the Sermon on the Mount; all there is concrete." But here we read in the same chapter with the Lord's Prayer such unconcrete expressions as these: "If therefore the light that is in thee be darkness, how great is the darkness!" (ver. 23); "Ye cannot serve God and mammon" (24); "Seek ye first his kingdom and his righteousness" (33). Even the golden rule is a wonderfully broad generalization. Now it is the glory of the New Testament that it is practical, simple, direct, but surely there is no such slavery to the concrete as to give even a presumption, in any single passage, in favor of the rendering "evil one" over "evil."

4. The comparative frequency of the use in the New Testament of the masculine and neuter of πονηρός. Lightfoot says (p. 280) "ὁ πονηρός occurs three or four times

as often as τὸ πονηρόν." Taking the author's own examples, we find that this generalization, converted into its particulars, is this: The masculine is used seven times, and the neuter twice, and possibly four times more, for there are four examples doubtful (pp. 274, 275). Add to this the fact that the neuter κακόν is used constantly without important difference from πονηρόν. E. g., Rom. xii. has τὸ πονηρόν in the ninth verse, and τὸ κακόν in the twenty-first, both in opposition to τὸ ἀγαθόν. For some reason the masculine κακός is seldom used in the New Testament.

5. The antithesis between μὴ εἰσενέγκῃς εἰς πειρασμόν and ἀλλὰ ῥῦσαι ἡμᾶς ἀπὸ τοῦ πονηροῦ. Lightfoot says (p. 289): "If the tempter is mentioned in the second clause, then, and then only, has the connection μή—ἀλλά—its proper force. If, on the other hand, τοῦ πονηροῦ be taken neuter, the strong opposition implied by these particles is no longer natural, for 'temptation' is not co-extensive with 'evil.' We should rather expect in this case '*And* deliver us from evil.'" But is not this making too much of μή—ἀλλά—? It is safe to say that in Greek (though the like would not be quite true of Latin) οὐκ (μή)—ἀλλά is used properly whenever "not—but—" could be used in English. And has the English mind ever felt any infelicity of connection in the common rendering "Lead us *not* into temptation, *but* deliver us from evil"? "Bring us not into solicitations to evil, but deliver us from it." Certainly οὐκ—ἀλλά—does not require the clauses to be very exact counterparts. Examples of a looser antith-

esis could easily be produced, if it were necessary. Here are two from Matthew: οὐκ ἔχει δὲ ῥίζαν ἐν ἑαυτῷ, ἀλλὰ πρόσκαιρός ἐστιν (xiii. 21); οὐκ ἐπέγνωσαν αὐτόν, ἀλλ' ἐποίησαν ἐν αὐτῷ ὅσα ἠθέλησαν (xvii. 12). In both these καὶ διὰ τοῦτο might have been used instead of ἀλλά, but surely both are right, as they are. The word "temptation" does at once suggest the tempter, but not necessarily the *mention* of the tempter. That might be dispensed with, as being fully implied, and the thought in the second clause advanced and broadened to deliverance from all the forms and power of sin which the tempter promotes.

6. The omission by Luke of the clause beginning with ἀλλά. Whether τοῦ πονηροῦ be masculine or neuter, he might omit this clause as practically involved in the preceding. The neuter does not make the second clause an independent petition. Luke's petition is virtually: "Deliver us from temptation to evil," and thus his record involves abridgment, but not serious curtailment. Luke gives us "Thy kingdom come," and omits "Thy will be done, as in heaven, so on earth." The petition omitted may be called merely an expansion of the preceding, but it is nearer being an independent petition than "Deliver us from evil."

7. A possible reference to the temptation of Christ in the wilderness. Dr. Chase says (p. 104): "Every clause of the Prayer, I believe, stands forth with greater sharpness and clearness of meaning when seen in the light of the Lord's Temptation." A general criticism of Dr.

DOES THE LORD'S PRAYER MENTION THE DEVIL? 89

Chase's most thorough and valuable discussion would be that he inclines to connect the phraseology of the Prayer with almost everything that is important in the New Testament. He is not alone, however, in associating τοῦ πονηροῦ with the temptation. Lightfoot says (p. 290): "Nor is it an insignificant fact that, only two chapters before, St. Matthew has recorded how the Author of this prayer found himself face to face with temptation (iv. 1, 3), and was delivered from the Evil One." But this same St. Matthew in recording, "only two chapters before," the temptation calls the tempter once ὁ πειράζων (verse 3), four times ὁ διάβολος (verses 1, 5, 8, 11), and not once ὁ πονηρός, "the evil one." For we must not forget that the question is not merely whether Jesus was thinking of the Tempter in the wilderness, a question too deep for us, but whether Matthew's verbal usage favors the meaning "Evil One." Why should he not use one of the two words employed "only two chapters before"?

8. The use of πονηροῦ instead of some other word for evil. It is claimed that if πονηροῦ means moral evil, a better word could have been chosen, as ἁμαρτία, πονηρία, ἀνομία. It is not always possible to show why a writer or speaker does not choose some different word. Nor is it necessary to prove that he chooses the best word. But in this case it is easy to see that ἁμαρτία would fail to carry the suggestion of harm and loss which τὸ πονηρόν does, and that ἀνομία is more restricted in meaning. In regard to πονηρία, which Matthew uses but once, or κακία, these also, as abstracts, are less suggestive of

the evil fruits of wickedness than τὸ πονηρόν. The latter would be more likely, I think, to be used by one who felt and feared the curse of sin. Nor should it be forgotten that τὸ πονηρόν is broad enough to embrace not only all evil conduct, but all evil influences, and all evil Ones.

9. The early versions, particularly the Latin and Syriac. In addition to the fact that no version, early or late, is authoritative, we find that the Latin, both Old Latin and Vulgate, simply adopts the ambiguity of the Greek—"Libera nos a malo." It is true that in the First Epistle of John whenever πονηρός refers to Satan it is translated "malignus," but this cannot be made the rule. Matt. xiii. 19 has "Venit malus et rapit quod seminatum est." At first glance, the Syriac, both Curetonian and Peshitto, seems to decide in favor of "Evil One," for the word is masculine; but when we remember that the Syriac, like the other Semitic languages, has no neuter gender, and sometimes uses the masculine for abstracts, this evidence is considerably weakened. The late Dr. Isaac H. Hall, a recognized authority in Syriac scholarship, wrote to me in 1891: "As to the Peshitto, perhaps different people would argue differently from the same data. I think, however, that it favors the rendering 'evil.' Adjectives used as abstract nouns prefer the feminine form, both where the Latin uses the neuter plural and neuter singular, but this is by no means the universal usage. It prevails rather in extra-biblical and later Syriac. The masculine is common enough for abstracts of every

sort. The Lord's Prayer has the masculine, which is used in very many places in the Peshitto for the neuter, even in rendering other words than πονηρόν. So far as I have read Syriac, the writers generally—I refer to allusions only—look upon the phrase as 'evil,' not 'the evil one.'"

10. The opinions and diction of the Greek Fathers. It cannot be disputed that these Fathers interpreted τοῦ πονηροῦ as the Evil One, Satan. Says Lightfoot (p. 307): "Among *Greek* writers there is, so far as I have observed, absolute unanimity on this point. They do not even betray the slightest suspicion that any other interpretation is possible." Again (p. 319): "To sum up; the earliest Latin Father [this is much more effective than to say," The erratic Tertullian"], and the earliest Greek Father of whose opinions we have any knowledge, both take τοῦ πονηροῦ masculine.* The masculine rendering seems to have been adopted universally by the Greek Fathers. At least no authority, even of a late date, has been produced for the neuter. In the Latin Church the earliest distinct testimony for the neuter is St. Augustine, at the end of the fourth and the beginning of the fifth century. From that time forward the neuter gained ground in the Western Church till it altogether supplanted the masculine." Again (p. 314): "With Augustine, however, a new era begins. The voice of the original Greek has ceased to be heard, or at least to be heard by an ear familiar with its idiom;

---

*Yet Clemens Romanus prays (Corinthians, 60) ῥυσθῆναι ἀπὸ πάσης ἁμαρτίας, in language that seems to echo the Lord's Prayer. So Dr. Charles Taylor in the Guardian, Jan. 6, 1897.

and, notwithstanding his spiritual insight, the loss here, as elsewhere, is very perceptible." It is further claimed, though not, I think, by Lightfoot, that the usage and diction of the Greek Fathers are evidence, independent of their interpretation, in favor of the masculine. In other words, they constantly refer to Satan as "the evil one" in other connections than in the Lord's Prayer, and are therefore independent witnesses to the linguistic usage.

In regard to the exegesis of the early Fathers it is needless to bring proof that in judgment and acumen they are inferior to modern interpreters and to some of the later Fathers. The only points worth considering are whether their nearness to apostolic times, or their intimate knowledge of Greek and "an ear familiar with its idiom," makes them reliable guides. On this last point it is enough to say that the gender of τοῦ πονηροῦ is not a question of Greek idiom. Masculine and neuter are both equally good Greek. Also, the logical connection cannot be determined by linguistic evidence. To say that St. Augustine had lost the delicate sense of Greek idiom—but he was familiar with Greek—I cannot think to be important. Indeed, an imperfect acquaintance with Greek would have inclined him to the masculine because of the un-Latin-like idiom of the article with the neuter. The Vulgate has the ambiguous rendering "a malo." A poor Greek scholar would have put it—as Beza, who was not a poor Greek scholar, did, following the Greek Fathers,— "ab illo malo." It simply cannot be that the Fathers favored the masculine on account of Greek idiom.

As to the independent value of the diction of the Fathers, it might be said that their usage simply grew out of their exegesis, but I will not insist on this. Let it stand that both in exegesis and in general usage the Greek Fathers unequivocally favor the masculine. Let us refrain too from thinking that their unanimity was owing to the overwhelming influence of Origen. Admitting all that is claimed in regard to their interpretation, their usage, and their opportunities of traditional light from the primitive Christian years, we have yet to set down two important facts.

First, the diction of the Fathers in the use of πονηρός is different from that of the New Testament. A striking illustration of this is found in the passage quoted by Bishop Lightfoot (p. 307) from the Clementine Homilies. In the dialogue between Simon the Samaritan and St. Peter (Hom. xix. 2) the question is sharply raised whether Satan really exists. I translate, restoring the lines omitted by the Bishop. Peter says: "I acknowledge that the Evil One exists, because the Master, who spoke the truth in everything, often said that he existed. At the outset he acknowledges that for forty days he by word of mouth tempted him. And elsewhere I know that he said: 'If Satan cast out Satan he is divided against himself; how, then, can his kingdom stand?' Also he declared that he saw the Evil One as lightning fall from heaven. And in another place he said: 'He that sowed the bad seed is the devil.' And again: 'Give no occasion to the Evil One.' Further, by way of counsel he said: 'Let your language be Yea, Yea, and Nay, Nay, but what is more than these is from the Evil One.' Further, in the Prayer which he handed down we have it said, 'Deliver us from the Evil One.' And in another place he pledged himself to say to the ungodly: 'Depart into the outer darkness, which the Father prepared for the devil and his angels.' And, not to prolong what I have to say, I know that my Master often said that the Evil One exists."* These few lines contain six instances of the masculine πονηρός applied to Satan. What is more, there are two quotations from the New Testament in which ὁ πονηρός *is substituted* for the New Testament words. The passage in Luke (x. 18), "I beheld Satan fall as lightning from heaven," appears thus: ‘Εώρακεν τὸν πονηρὸν ὡς ἀστραπὴν πεσόντα. A passage from Paul (Eph. iv. 27)—we need not blame this Father, whoever he was, for forgetting that Paul said it instead of Jesus—"Neither give place to the devil," is given, almost unrecognizable, it is true, Μὴ δότε πρόφασιν τῷ πονηρῷ.† In two other quotations Σατανᾶς and διάβολος remain unchanged. We can imagine what a transformation would have been wrought in Matthew's record of the Temptation and elsewhere, if this writer had taken the place of the first evangelist. It should be added that the neuter τὸ πονηρόν is found at least twice in the same Homily (chap. 20).

The second important fact is one of theological opinion, viz., that the Fathers, in their thinking, gave more promi-

---

*Ed. Dressel, p. 372.

†Dressel in his note says: "Testimonium forsan Ebionitici evangelii, affine dicto apostolico."

nence to Satan than the New Testament does. This is shown first by the theory of the atonement held by even so early a Father as Irenæus. Imagine Peter and Paul preaching and writing that the sufferings and death of Christ were a ransom paid to the devil for our release. Says Shedd, speaking of the writings of the first three centuries, "It is very plain that in seizing so rankly, as the theological mind of this age did, upon those few texts in which the connection and relations of Satan with the work of Christ are spoken of, and allowing them to eclipse those far more numerous passages in which the Redeemer's work is exhibited in its reference to the being and attributes of God, it was liable to a one-sided construction of the doctrine." Again, "The claims of God and of the attribute of justice were thrown too much into the background by those of Satan."*

The patristic theory of the atonement is sufficient to prove the deviation of the Fathers from the sobriety and truth of our Lord and his apostles. But we may put beside this the great importance attached to exorcism. Evil spirits, subjects of "the evil one," must be cast out by rites and ceremonies. Early in the third century exorcism began to be connected with baptism, and thus virtually became a sacrament of the church.

Now all this subserviency to Satan seemed to the early Fathers genuine Christianity; but we see it to be exaggeration and perversion. And is it not plain that minds breathing such a theological atmosphere as they did would

---

*"History of Christian Doctrine," Vol. ii., pp. 215, 266.

inevitably interpret ambiguous passages of the New Testament so as to magnify the agency of Satan? Why then should we follow their guidance under the notion that somehow "the voice of the original Greek" taught them the true meaning?

Enough of indecisive considerations. Some will perhaps see in them a cumulative result of slight probabilities in favor of one or the other of the disputed renderings, but I am sure that most students of the subject will say that it is hopeless to look for a decision on these indeterminate grounds. It seems to me, however, that there is some hope of a decision, in the answer to this simple question, too much neglected in this discussion, viz., Was ὁ πονηρός the usual term to designate the devil? If not, then we should not expect to find it in such a formula of devotion as the Lord's Prayer. Now the moment this question is raised, it answers itself in the mind of one who is familiar with the New Testament. Such a one will feel, without resorting to exegetical statistics—often a poor resort—how changed the gospel narrative would be if certain well-remembered passages should read thus: "Then was Jesus led up of the Spirit into the wilderness to be tempted of the *evil one*;" "And when the *evil one* came to him, he said, If thou be the Son of God," etc.; "Then the *evil one* leaveth him, and behold angels came;" "The enemy that sowed them [the tares] is the *evil one*;" "Depart from me, ye cursed, into everlasting fire, prepared for the *evil one* and his angels;" "How can the *evil one* cast out the *evil one*?"

DOES THE LORD'S PRAYER MENTION THE DEVIL? 97

"Then entered the *evil one* into Judas;" "Ye are of your father, the *evil one;*" "The *evil one* cometh and hath nothing in me"! In these and in more than a score of other passages in the Gospels, which strike one as containing the principal references to the Devil, the original words are διάβολος, Σατανᾶς, ὁ πειράζων, ἄρχων τοῦ κόσμου. Outside of the Gospels the usual words are διάβολος and Σατανᾶς.

It is not denied that sometimes ὁ πονηρός means the Devil. No one supposes that it always does. An example both of the masculine, denoting a man, and of the neuter abstract is in Luke vi. 45: ὁ πονηρὸς ἐκ τοῦ πονηροῦ [θησαυροῦ] προφέρει τὸ πονηρόν. So in 1 Cor. v. 13, Ἐξάρατε τὸν πονηρὸν ἐξ ὑμῶν αὐτῶν, rendered in the Revision, "Put away the wicked man from among yourselves." Also in Matt. v. 39, the Revision reads, "Resist not him that is evil" (τῷ πονηρῷ). It would hardly do to translate "Resist not the evil one," with the ἀντίστητε δὲ τῷ διαβόλῳ, καὶ φεύξεται ἀφ' ὑμῶν of James iv. 7 before us.

How many are the clear and certain cases of ὁ πονηρός meaning Satan? If we set aside those passages in which "evil" finds a place in the margin of the Revision (Matt. v. 37; vi. 13; John xvii. 15; 2 Thess. iii. 3), we have, as claimed, the following: Matt. xiii. 19, 38; Eph. vi. 16; 1 John ii. 13, 14; iii. 12; v. 18, 19. Of these, Matt. xiii. 38 is, Ὁ δὲ ἀγρός ἐστιν ὁ κόσμος· τὸ δὲ καλὸν σπέρμα, οὗτοί εἰσιν οἱ υἱοὶ τῆς βασιλείας· τὰ δὲ ζιζάνιά εἰσιν οἱ υἱοὶ τοῦ πονηροῦ. Probably the reason why "evil" was not put in the margin was that the common version had "children of the wicked one," there being, therefore, no occasion for marginal concession or conciliation; but is it not true, as Cremer suggests, that the parallel phrase, υἱοὶ τῆς βασιλείας, requires the rendering "sons of evil"? It should be noted that in the words immediately following, the Devil is mentioned by his usual name, and is said to be the sower of the tares and the enemy of him who sowed the good seed. Thus we have two antitheses—the Lord and Satan, good men and evil men; and the antithesis is sharper and much more natural with a single mention of Satan as the antagonist of Jesus. The Hebraism "sons of evil" would be as natural as "son of hell" (Matt. xxiii. 15); "sons of disobedience" (Eph. v. 6); and the "son of worthlessness [Belial]" of the Old Testament.

Another passage in the above list is 1 John v. 19, Ὁ κόσμος ὅλος ἐν τῷ πονηρῷ κεῖται, rendered in the Revision "the whole world lieth in the evil one," with no "evil" in the alternative margin. But does it not require a strong effort to suppress the sense of incongruity in the rendering "lieth in the evil one," when "in evil" is not only grammatical, but harmonizes fully with "evil one" mentioned in the previous verse? Compare the τοῦ πονηροῦ and πονηρά of iii. 12. Such expressions as "Abide *in* me;" "them which are *in* Christ Jesus;" "one body *in* Christ;" "fallen asleep *in* Christ;" "life hid with Christ *in* God;" "We are *in* him that is true" (ver. 20)—expressions so numerous in the New Testament, especially in John, as in the allegory of the vine, imply an all-pervading presence which the Scriptures nowhere ascribe

DOES THE LORD'S PRAYER MENTION THE DEVIL? 99

to the Devil, leader of all evil agents and agencies though he be. The "in" of such profound phraseology is very different from the ἐν instrumental of Matt. xii. 24, "This man doth not cast out devils, but in Beelzebub the prince of the devils."

I will venture, then, to subtract two from the list given above, leaving six in the whole New Testament, and *one only* in the four Gospels (Matt. xiii. 19). That one is indisputable, because assured by the parallel passages in Mark and Luke. In the parable of the sower, where Matthew says: "Ἔρχεται ὁ πονηρὸς καὶ ἁρπάζει τὸ ἐσπαρμένον;" Mark says: "Ἔρχεναι ὁ Σατανᾶς (iv. 15); Luke says: "Ἔρχεται ὁ διάβολος (viii. 12). If we had a similar parallelism in the Lord's Prayer, there would be no need of discussion. The most that we can say, in comparing the evangelists, is that Mark never uses ὁ πονηρός at all, and Luke never uses ὁ πονηρός for Satan, but always διάβολος or Σατανᾶς, and that he once uses the neuter τὸ πονηρόν, and that too in his Sermon on the Mount. Compare Luke vi. 45 with Matt. vii. 18. But while spending our time in debating whether Satan is called "the evil one" just seven times, or six, or five, we are apt to forget that more than seventy times he is called by other names, almost always Satan or Devil. All the undoubted examples of the term "evil one" except two are in the First Epistle of John. In the Gospels there is but one, viz., Matt. xiii. 19, this being given by only one of the three reporting evangelists. If we were not in a serious discussion, I should be tempted to call it one-third of an example, because probably, either by varying tradition or by deliberate choice of the writers, the three words came from the same Aramaic source. Now while it is *possible* that this rare usage should be incorporated into such a formula as the Lord's Prayer, it seems to me extremely improbable. The presumption is strongly against it.

This strong presumption is confirmed, and made almost a certainty, by Old Testament usage. The Septuagint has frequent use of πονηρόν and κακόν, with, and sometimes without, the article, to denote evil in general. The first reference to evil is in Gen. ii. 9—τὸ ξύλον τοῦ εἰδέναι γνωστὸν καλοῦ καὶ πονηροῦ. In Deut. iv. 25, we read: ἐὰν ποιήσητε τὸ πονηρὸν ἐνώπιον κυρίου, and this language is so reiterated in the books that follow, that doing "evil in the sight of the Lord" rings like a sad refrain all through the history. The Psalms and prophets continue the same usage. David's lament in the penitential Psalm—σοὶ μόνῳ ἥμαρτον, καὶ τὸ πονηρὸν ἐνώπιόν σου ἐποίησα (li. 4. (1.6))—and Isaiah's οὐαὶ οἱ λέγοντες τὸ πονηρὸν καλόν (v. 20) are examples. We base no argument on the fact that Satan is never called "the evil one" in the Old Testament. We do not place Old Testament usage on a level with that of the New Testament on this point. Whatever may be the reason, the doctrine of Satan is mostly a New Testament doctrine, but the notion of evil in general is common and impressive in the Old Testament, and is very often expressed in the Septuagint by τὸ πονηρόν. The Old Testament all bears one way on the question before us. We would not limit all the words of our Lord to Old Testament meanings, but his hearers were familiar with the idea of evil itself as a dreadful reality. It was a part of their biblical training, and we may well believe that divine wisdom did not overlook this in giving form to that comprehensive guide to prayer. Indeed, if we do not greatly overestimate the influence of the Old Testament on the minds of serious Jews, we may say that, unless the language employed by our Lord was decisively limited to an evil *person*, his hearers would inevitably understand it of evil itself. In all this we do not forget that the Septuagint is a translation, and that a large part of the Gospels is virtually the same. The argument from the Old Testament is from the idea of evil, and not from any particular word to express it. It may be added, however, that in the Hebrew Old Testament the article is almost always used with רַע (הָרַע) to express "evil" substantively—that which is evil. Still further, of all the Evangelists, Matthew—Luke's genuine text does not contain the petition—is most under the influence of Old Testament ideas, as is shown by the great number of his citations.

The force of all this is not much weakened by the fact that Satan is not often spoken of by any name in the Old Testament, nor by the greater prominence given to the agency of Satan in later times. Lightfoot says (p. 282): "The Septuagint version of the Old Testament was made two or three centuries before the Gospels were written. This interval was a period of constant and rapid development. Theological nomenclature moved forward with the movement of the ages. Terms wholly unknown at the beginning of this period were in everybody's mouth at the end." But the influence of the Old Testament on the minds of Christ's hearers in regard to "evil" did not depend on the frequency or infrequency of the mention of Satan, or on the diction of the Septuagint, but on the positive and ever-present power of those writings which were "read in the synagogues every Sabbath," and taught in every devout family. No doubt, new terms arose, but they must have arisen slowly, and have supplanted others still more slowly, and if any term ever clearly had the field to express wicked conduct, it was in our Savior's time, "evil," in whatever language it may have been clothed; while "evil one" was, it is true, beginning to be used occasionally as a name of the Devil.

In this connection I ought, perhaps, to refer to the Talmud, the knowledge of which, it has been said, is mostly disseminated by quoting from quotations. The Talmud might have been put with emphasis in the list of our indecisive sources of evidence; for it contains the petitions "Deliver us from evil" and "Deliver us from Satan," and a special search was rewarded by the discovery of three passages in which Satan was called the Wicked One. These may be found on pages 285, 286, in Lightfoot's Appendix II. I will make short work of the immense and almost inaccessible Talmud, because I know so little about it, but I have read carefully a little volume, the orthodox Jewish Prayer-book, and perhaps its ancient prayers represent the devotions of the time of Christ as correctly as the Talmud, which in its earliest written portions is two centuries after Christ. Among these ancient prayers, none of which make mention of the evil one, we find in the Morning Service the following: "O Lord, have pity on thy people Israel, and deliver us from all evil."* "Lead us not into the power of sin, transgressions, iniquity, temptation, or contempt. Suffer not the evil imagination to have dominion over us; and remove far from us evil men and wicked associates and works." But the Talmud, it seems, adds to such prayers as these the petition: "Deliver us from Satan." Now, if the question were, Did the ancient Jews pray to be delivered from Satan *or* from evil? then the Talmud would answer, They prayed for deliverance from *both*. After all, I do not believe that the Talmud has very much to do with the question what the Lord's Prayer means. If it gave us the exact petition "Deliver us from the evil one," how much would its evidence be worth against that derived from the Old Testament?

Our conclusion, then, is that in the Lord's Prayer we are taught to say, "Deliver us from evil"—a petition that reaches to the lowest depths of weak, sinful human nature. If it could be shown that "evil one" was a common designation of the Devil, even then there would be no preponderance in favor of the rendering, "Deliver us from the evil one." The case would be simply evenly balanced so far as the language itself is concerned; and the weight of

---

* הַצִּילֵנוּ מִכָּל רָע, which may be rendered in Greek, $\rho\tilde{v}\sigma\alpha\iota\ \dot{\eta}\mu\tilde{\alpha}\varsigma\ \dot{\alpha}\pi\dot{o}\ \pi\alpha\nu\tau\dot{o}\varsigma\ \pi o\nu\eta\rho o\tilde{v}$. Compare Ps. cxxi. (cxx.) 7, $K\dot{v}\rho\iota o\varsigma\ \varphi v\lambda\dot{\alpha}\xi\alpha\iota\ \sigma\varepsilon\ \dot{\alpha}\pi\dot{o}\ \pi\alpha\nu\tau\dot{o}\varsigma\ \kappa\alpha\kappa o\tilde{v}$.

evidence from the Old Testament would be decisive. But when we think how seldom the name "evil one" was applied to Satan, and that this ought to have considerable weight in every instance of ambiguity, and especial weight in interpreting a prayer remarkable for its simplicity and directness, then our conclusion seems well-nigh certain.

IV

DOES ἡλικία, IN MATTHEW AND LUKE, MEAN STATURE OR AGE?

Τίς δὲ ἐξ ὑμῶν μεριμνῶν δύναται προσθεῖναι ἐπὶ τὴν ἡλικίαν αὐτοῦ πῆχυν ἕνα; Matt. vi. 27. Compare Luke xii. 25.

IN classical usage the meaning "stature" is rare. The best lexicons refer us to only five examples, and two of these are erroneous. In Plutarch, a contemporary of John, there seems to be not a single example, though he uses ἡλικία many times. There is one clear case in Herodotus (iii., 16). After describing the indignities inflicted on the dead body of Amasis by Cambyses, he says that the Egyptians asserted that it was not Amasis but a certain Egyptian of the same stature—*ἔχων τὴν αὐτὴν ἡλικίην Ἀμάσι*. Demosthenes furnishes another example in one of the "testimonies" appended to his oration "Adversus Bœotum" (1024). In speaking of his daughter the witness says that if you look at her stature—*τὴν δ' ἡλικίαν αὐτῆς ἂν ἴδητε*—you would suppose her to be his sister. Again, Lucian in his True History—the ancient Gulliver's Travels—speaks of men, though he admits it to be *παραδοξότατον*, of about half-furlong statures—*ἡμισταδιαίους τὰς ἡλικίας*.

The Septuagint, Canon and Apocrypha, has but one example of "stature" (Ezek. xiii. 18), and that one we could not be sure of, if we did not know the original Hebrew.

Coming to the New Testament, where ἡλικία is used eight times, one of these a mere repetition (John ix. 23), we find but one case that is not disputed—the ἡλικία of Zacchæus—although Eph. iv. 13 seems to me almost as clear. Paul had just been speaking of "the *building up of the body of Christ*," and he adds, "till we all attain . . . unto a full-grown man, of the stature (ἡλικίας) of the fullness of Christ." Luke ii. 52 may fairly be considered doubtful, especially on account of the verb προέκοπτεν, which would not go so well with "stature" as with "maturity of age." This leaves two cases of the undisputed meaning "age," that of the blind man healed, who was "of age" (John ix. 21, 23), and Sarah, who was "past age" (Heb. xi. 11).

Usage, then, by a majority vote favors the meaning "age," but there are examples enough of the meaning "stature" to allow the passages before us to be settled purely by connection of thought. Which best suits the immediate and surrounding context? There is no doubt that the first impression is in favor of applying "cubit" to stature. The older commentators seem to have followed this, and I think it is a case where first impressions should rule. Bengel makes short work of the other view— "Hanc [aetatem] nemo cubitis metitur" (note on Luke xii. 25). It must be admitted that the most eminent modern commentators have abandoned this first impression. Tholuck in his "Sermon on the Mount" refers to

Ps. xxxix. 5, Job ix. 25, Acts xiii. 25, 2 Tim. iv. 7, in favor of "age," and, in extra-Biblical Greek, to Diogenianus, Alcæus and Mimnermus. Meyer gives the first and last of these, but Alford gives all except Acts xiii. 25, including the misprint in Tholuck for Diogenianus. With all respect for these distinguished names, it must be said that such parallel references are utterly misleading, and tend to throw discredit on all usage-study; for (1) the "hand-breadth" of the Psalm, the "finger-breadth" of Alcæus, and the "cubit-time" ($\pi \eta \chi \upsilon \iota o \nu \; \chi \rho \acute{o} \nu o \nu$) of Mimnermus are obvious poetic diction, and one of the elementary principles of usage-study is not to mix and confound poetry and prose. (2) Still more unfit is the comparison with Job's saying, "My days are swifter than a post," and the reference to $\delta \rho \acute{o} \mu o \varsigma$ in the Acts and 2 Tim. ("John was fulfilling his *course*," "I have finished my *course*"). What is the use of studying usage at all, if we must put together such incongruous notions on the general ground, of course indisputable, that words of space are often applied to time?

If, then, the joining of cubit to age is unsupported by usage, how is it about the context? Meyer and Alford insist that the connection demands "age"; "for," says the latter, "the object of food and clothing is not to *enlarge the body*, but to prolong life." Let us look at verses 25-28. "Be not anxious for your life, what ye shall eat, or what ye shall drink; nor yet for your body, what ye shall put on. Is not the life more than the food, and the body than the raiment? Behold the birds of the heaven

. . . your heavenly Father feedeth them. . . . Which of you by being anxious can add one cubit unto his stature? And why are ye anxious concerning raiment? Consider the lilies of the field," etc. Here are mentioned two objects of anxiety, food and clothing—food for the life, and clothing for the body. Life is more than food, and the body than raiment. The Father who gives life will give its needful food, and he who gives the body will give its needed clothing. There are two pairs, life and food, body and raiment. Now the discussion of the first pair closes, I think, with the 26th verse, "Are not ye of much more value than they?" Next begins (and the δέ after τίς favors this) the second pair, body and raiment. The 27th verse is a fit opening for this, but is it a fitting close for the preceding? The body is God's gift, and he will provide clothing for it. He gives it as it is, and we cannot change its stature by our anxiety. No more need is there of our being anxious about its clothing.

In Luke (xii. 22-29) we find the same two pairs, and the verse about the cubit serves equally well for an introduction to the second. Instead of Matthew's καὶ περὶ ἐνδύματος τί μεριμνᾶτε; where καί, according to its New Testament inclusiveness, nearly equals οὖν, Luke has εἰ οὖν οὐδὲ ἐλάχιστον δύνασθε, τί περὶ τῶν λοιπῶν μεριμνᾶτε; Omitting the word for clothing, he implies it in "the rest," and goes on, like Matthew, with the beautiful parable-argument from the lilies. His εἰ οὖν fastens the connection of the "cubit" verse to the following instead of the preceding. Meyer and Alford find an objection to the meaning "stature" in the word ἐλάχιστον, the latter saying that a cubit would be "a very large increase." But why emphasize πῆχυν after this mechanical fashion? Our Savior's argument would have been the same if he had said "inch" or "hair-breadth." Plainly, "cubit" was used as a common unit of measure. The substance of the thought was that man cannot change the stature that God has given him. Also difference in height of body is a very small matter (ἐλάχιστον) compared with the care of the body, whether short or tall. Further, it may be that οὐδὲ ἐλάχιστον is to be taken adverbially—"you are able not even in the least" to increase the stature.

Another objection is drawn from the grotesqueness of even suggesting a cubit's increase in stature. Bengel is not disturbed by this; he says, "ut fiat giganti similis." Meyer considers the notion "sehr unpassend." So it might be, if the language implied the possible desirableness of adding a cubit to *all* men's stature. But the absurdity vanishes when we think of the *differences* in men's height, and that while some would not care to be taller, others might. The very form of the question suggests individuals: "Which of you?" Our Savior may have had among his hearers a Saul, of whom it is said, "From his shoulders and upward he was taller than any of the people" (1 Sam. ix. 2.), and a Zacchæus, whom all the world knows to have been "little of stature" (τῇ ἡλικίᾳ μικρός—Luke xix. 3). We do not know the exact height of either, but there must have been a difference of more than a cubit. One naturally thinks of the pet regiment of Frederick William I. of Prussia, in which some of the men were seven feet tall, while the statement is made that the requirement for the Japanese army is only 4 feet 11. If something more accurate is wanted, it can be found in gymnasium records; but almost any one, without going to formal records, can find among his acquaintances men who are 6 feet 4, and others under 5 feet. All this would not be worth the while except to answer an objection, for, as has been said already, the cubit was mentioned as a common unit of measure,—as we use foot and inch—and not for mathematical exactness.

Let it be added here that the objections are not all on one side. Besides the objection to "age" from the incongruity of the connection with "cubit," it may be said that one can by care prolong his life. The suggestion that he cannot, so fixed are the limits of life by God's purpose, gives a prominence to Divine foreordination that is out of harmony with the occasion, with the Sermon on the Mount, and with the general teaching of Jesus.

We may come back, then, with confidence to our first impression in favor of the rendering "stature." A careful examination of the passage confirms the verdict of plain common sense, the judgment of the older commentators, and the rendering of the oldest versions, viz., the Old Latin, the Old Syriac, and, if we may trust a translation of a translation, the Gospel-harmony of Tatian.

V

TO THE SLEEPING DISCIPLES

Καθεύδετε τὸ λοιπὸν καὶ ἀναπαύεσθε. Mark xiv. 41.
Compare Matt. xxvi. 45, 46; Luke xxii. 45, 46.

IT has been much discussed whether Jesus used this language in earnest, or in irony, as if saying, "Sleep on, if you can in such an hour as this." If used in earnest, how could he say immediately, "Arise, let us be going"? Perhaps all that is needed is to read the whole narrative of the Agony in the garden, with the eyes of the imagination wide open. Three times Jesus went a short distance from the three disciples, that he might endure the agony alone, yet not far from sympathy. Twice he returned and awoke them from a sleep which he kindly excused. He returns the third time. Does he awake them again? Not at once. Looking with eyes of pity on the forlorn "o'erwatched" friends, he speaks a few tender words to ears that do not hear. It is more a soliloquy. "Sleep henceforth and take rest: it is enough: the hour is come; behold, the Son of man is betrayed into the hands of sinners." The loving Heart anticipates their relief from the dreadful strain. He speaks, but they do not hear, until with sharp tones of urgent necessity he cries out, "Arise, let us be going," and, as they rouse themselves to obey, he repeats in substance what he had already said unheard, "Behold, he that betrayeth me is at hand."

VI

DEMONS

Κύριε, καὶ τὰ δαιμόνια ὑποτάσσεται ἡμῖν ἐν τῷ ὀνόματί σου.
—Luke x. 17.

What were demons, or devils, as our versions call them? Were they real or imaginary? These questions annoy exegesis without being properly in its sphere. Exegesis says: "They were, in the opinion of the times, malignant spirits controlling and perverting men's minds, and making them what we now call crazy." Present opinion considers their victims to be simply mentally diseased. But this change of opinion need not trouble any reader of the New Testament when he comes to the accounts of demoniacal possession. The people of that day had their theory and we have ours, and how much will the men of the coming centuries care for either? For how much do we know absolutely of mental disease, or affections of the brain? Suppose some one should extend the germ-theory of disease so as to cover all brain-ailments, and people the head with a legion of living pests, could the nineteenth, or twentieth, century in the West say much in scorn of the first century in the East? Nor in fact have we altogether given up its way of speaking, for we sometimes say a man is "possessed." At any rate the notion of devils in a human being is respectable enough to be read of without distress or disgust, as an ancient theory of frenzy or madness. Exegesis calmly acknowledges that there was no other way to speak of the matter at that time and in that place. Jesus himself not only assumed human nature, but entered into the mind of the times. There is no need of explaining his words by an "accommodation theory" of adapting his language to the ignorance of his hearers. Is it not utterly idle to set up a duplex analysis of the intellectual experience of the God-man? The incarnation, of itself, was an all-inclusive "accommodation" to our earthly life.

VII

THE NEW TESTAMENT USE OF ἀγαπάω AND φιλέω

'Αγαπᾷς με; . . . φιλῶ σε. . . . ἀγαπᾷς με; . . . φιλῶ σε. . . . φιλεῖς με; ἐλυπήθη ὁ Πέτρος ὅτι εἶπεν αὐτῷ τὸ τρίτον· φιλεῖς με; καὶ λέγει αὐτῷ· κύριε, πάντα σὺ οἶδας, σὺ γινώσκεις ὅτι φιλῶ σε. John xxi. 15-17.

It is to be expected that in discussing these two words one will begin by quoting from Trench's "Synonyms of the New Testament." He says (I. 67, Am. Ed.) that φιλέω (amo) "is more instinctive, is more of the feelings, implies more passion," while ἀγαπάω (diligo) indicates esteem, choice, a sense of what is fit and due its object. He dwells on John xxi. 15-17 as illustrating the difference. 'Αγαπᾷς on the Lord's lips "sounds too cold" to satisfy Peter, and at last Jesus gratifies him by adopting his own word, φιλεῖς.

President Woolsey, in an article of the greatest value in the Andover Review (Aug., 1885), dissents from this interpretation of the dialogue, while acknowledging the correctness of Trench's view in general. He considers it "more probable that Peter felt his love to Christ to be too human, too much like a friend's love to a friend," to deserve the word ἀγαπάω.

In the Bibliotheca Sacra for July, 1889, President Ballantine gives a searching criticism to the views of Trench,

Woolsey and others, and comes to the conclusion that in Biblical Greek there is no difference in meaning between ἀγαπάω and φιλέω. I will not undertake to give a summary of this article, but will merely say that future investigators will have to reckon with President Ballantine.

Possibly the following remarks may throw a little additional light on this obscure matter.

1.   There is a presumption against absolute identity of meaning in the case of almost any two words. This presumption is increased if the words express decided or strong feeling. It is still further increased if, in any particular passage, the words have an antithetical position, or seem to have special attention called to them in any way.

2.   The difference in meaning may be very slight and yet real; for meaning covers not merely the intellectual analysis of a word, but its association, and various shades of impression.

3.   Many a writer fails to observe those distinctions in words which are sanctioned by the best usage. This may arise from a lack of literary cultivation, from negligence, from excited feeling, or purposely for some temporary reason. So also a writer may observe the nicest distinctions in some parts of his work and neglect them in others. There is a personal usage, as well as general.

4.   The fact that a word was being superseded by another would not prove that both were used without discrimination. Sometimes it might be the antique air itself that recommended it, as in the English "quoth" for "said," and "token" for "sign."

5. When a word after long fluctuation settles down in a narrow corner of its former usage, it is natural to see in its earlier uses a tendency towards the final use. According to that, φιλέω, meaning at last only "to kiss," might during its later previous history express distinctively fondness, tenderness, or devotion.

6. The classical usage of ἀγαπάω and φιλέω is not much disputed. The former is more like the Latin "diligo," the latter "amo," but the line is not sharply drawn except that φιλέω only means to kiss, this use being as early as Herodotus. Aristotle, after saying (Rhet. I., 11, 17) that to be loved is pleasant (τὸ φιλεῖσθαι ἡδύ), adds that "to be loved is to be held dear for one's own sake," τὸ δὲ φιλεῖσθαι ἀγαπᾶσθαί ἐστιν αὐτὸν δι' αὐτόν. The standard quotation from Dion Cassius (about A. D. 180) has peculiar interest because it is from the speech of Antony, and must, therefore, be virtually a translation from the Latin. He says of Cæsar (44, 48, 1): Ἐφιλήσατε αὐτὸν ὡς πατέρα, καὶ ἠγαπήσατε ὡς εὐεργέτην—"Ye loved him as a father, and held him dear as a benefactor"—where one can plainly see the Latin amabatis, diligebatis.

7. Much more important is the usage of the Septuagint. Here the prevailing word is ἀγαπάω, being found, including the Apocrypha, about 270 times. It has a wide range. Says Ballantine, speaking of the canonical books, "It is the word in constant use to express (1) God's love to man, (2) God's love for truth and other virtuous and worthy objects, (3) man's love for God, (4) man's love for salvation and worthy objects, (5) man's conscientious

love for man, (6) ordinary human friendship, (7) parental and filial affection, (8) the love of husband and wife, (9) impure sexual love, (10) man's love for cursing and other vices and sinful objects." (P. 527). Very different is it with φιλέω. Of the twenty-five times of its occurrence, fourteen times it means to kiss, translating the Hebrew נָשַׁק. Nine times it represents אָהַב, like ἀγαπάω, and expresses once Jacob's love for Joseph, twice the love of wisdom, four times—three times applied to Isaac—love for a certain food. Twice it is joined with ἀγαπάω (ἐγὼ τοὺς ἐμὲ φιλοῦντας ἀγαπῶ, Prov. viii. 17, and Hos. iii. 1). In no case does it exhibit any remarkable difference from ἀγαπάω. But this is very remarkable, that it is so nearly a discarded word, except in the sense of "kiss." In the Psalms, which echo throughout with love, it never appears; in the Proverbs rarely, and in Isaiah but once. Why this blight on φιλέω in the Septuagint? I can think of no reason but this, that the usage of the time had emphasized its meaning of "kiss," and the Seventy having chosen it to represent the Hebrew נָשַׁק, its unfitness for general use for love was increased. There being back of this a pressure from the fact that the original Hebrew mostly used but one word for love, it was inevitable that the one Greek word should be ἀγαπάω and not φιλέω; and if we make the distinction of higher and lower, the former is the higher word.

8. In passing to New Testament usage we might expect a still further repression of φιλέω from the influence of the Septuagint, but this is not true of the New

Testament as a whole. As its usage is composite, it is best to consider the writers separately.

Matthew uses ἀγαπάω eight times, always with a personal object, God, our neighbor, enemies, etc. He uses φιλέω five times, twice in one passage of loving father, mother, son or daughter more than Christ, twice of things, praying standing, and uppermost rooms, and once concerning the kiss of Judas. His usage is like that of the Septuagint.

Mark uses a verb for love only six times, four times in one passage (xii. 30-33) in regard to the commands to love God and our neighbor. Here ἀγαπάω is found, and the language of the commands follows (as in Matthew and Luke), with some variations, the Septuagint. This leaves the account of the man whom Jesus loved, as he looked upon him (ἀγαπάω), and the language of Judas, "Whomsoever I shall kiss" (φιλέω).

Luke uses the same word for kiss (xxii. 47) and only once besides (xx. 46), of those who "love greetings in the markets." He uses ἀγαπάω 13 times mostly parallel with Matthew, but also once (xi. 43), very noticeably, of loving chief seats and salutations. In the Acts Luke has no word for love, neither verb nor noun. The synoptic writers, then, follow in the main the usage of the Septuagint in discriminating against φιλέω; its use being sufficient to show that it was a part of their vocabulary, but on a lower plane of meaning than ἀγαπάω.

Before taking up the writings of John let us glance at other writers of the New Testament. Peter uses ἀγαπάω only; in the first epistle four times (i. 8, 22; ii. 17; iii. 10), and in the second once (ii. 15). "Whom not having seen ye love," "Love one another," "Love the brotherhood," "Would love life"—this a quotation from the Septuagint—"Loved the wages of unrighteousness." James has ἀγαπάω only, and three times, twice in repeating the thought "promised to them that love him" (i. 12, ii. 5) and once in the command to love our neighbor (ii. 8). The writer to the Hebrews uses ἀγαπάω only, both times in quotations from the Septuagint (i. 9; xii.6).

Paul goes even beyond the Septuagint in his preference—spontaneous, of course—for ἀγαπάω. It is found in all his epistles except Philippians, 1 Timothy, Titus and Philemon, and is most used in Ephesians—ten times. Φιλέω is found but twice, as against thirty-four, in all, of ἀγαπάω. In these two passages—"If any man love not the Lord Jesus Christ" (1 Cor. xvi. 22) and "Greet them that love us in the faith" (Tit. iii. 15)—I cannot see a shade of difference from ἀγαπάω, and I imagine that in both cases he was led to depart from his almost universal usage by the word φίλημα, which was associated in his mind with Christian greeting, and at the close of 1 Corinthians was used but a line before φιλεῖ.

Coming now to the "Apostle of love," we find that in his epistles ἀγαπάω only is used, and that thirty-one times uniformly and with enthusiastic iteration it carries its deep, serious meaning. In Revelation φιλέω is found twice; once of loving a lie (xxii. 15), also in the message to the Laodiceans—"As many as I love I rebuke and chasten" (iii. 19). Ἀγαπάω is used four times (i. 5, iii. 9, xii. 11, xx. 9).

Next, let us examine the Gospel, omitting the 21st chapter. Here, although φιλέω is used much less than ἀγαπάω—eight to thirty-three—we seem to see a complete breaking away from the Septuagint as to the comparative elevation and dignity of the two words. Not only is there the closest resemblance in meaning, but there are several remarkable parallel uses. Thus, "The Father loveth (ἀγαπᾷ) the Son" (iii. 35), and "The Father loveth (φιλεῖ) the Son" (v. 20). "He that loveth (ἀγαπᾷ) me shall be loved (ἀγαπηθήσεται) of my Father" (xiv. 21), and in the same discourse, further on, "The Father himself loveth (φιλεῖ) you, because ye have loved (πεφιλήκατε) me" (xvi. 27). "The disciple standing by whom he loved" (ἠγάπα) (xix. 26), and in the next chapter, "The other disciple whom Jesus loved" (ἐφίλει) (xx. 2). With these examples before us, can we hesitate to add another as a true parallel, though in the face of Trench's ingenious distinction, "He whom thou lovest (φιλεῖς) is sick" (xi. 3), with "How he loved (ἐφίλει) him" (xi. 36) and "Jesus loved (ἠγάπα) Martha and her sister and Lazarus." This leaves but two examples of φιλέω—"He that loveth his life" (xii. 25), and "The world would love its own" (xv. 19). We are not yet through with John's use of these words, but so far, the impression is made on my own mind that he is uncritical in verbal distinctions, and willing to duplicate words in order to avail himself of all the resources of the language in expressing his thought.

9. We ought now to be prepared to take up the last chapter of the Gospel and the dialogue between our Lord and Peter. A discussion of the style of this chapter, as evincing its substantial genuineness, may be found in the article of President Woolsey already referred to.

An important question arises at once, viz., whether this dialogue was spoken in Greek or in Aramaic. It is probable that the latter, the Palestinian Syriac, was the language employed; for, (1) being the true vernacular of the country, we should expect it generally in private conversation. Paul used it even in a public speech at Jerusalem (Acts xxi. 40). (2) The mode of addressing Peter indicates this. While the evangelist, writing in Greek, calls him Simon Peter, Jesus in all three questions calls him Simon (son) of John, i. e., Simon Bar-Jonah, as in Matt. xvi. 17, which is Aramaic. Now if the conversation was in Aramaic, then the word for love, which John varies so strikingly, was probably one and the same in every case. Some evidence of this comes from the Old Syriac version, reinforced by the Peshitto version. The former is assigned to about A. D. 150 and is therefore a good witness to the Aramaic of our Savior's time. The Curetonian fragments do not contain the last seven chapters of John, but the recently discovered Sinai Codex, fortunately, has the larger part of them, including the twenty-first chapter, with the loss of only a word or two in the 19th verse. In the interview with Peter only one word is used for love (in Hebrew characters רחם), and that in the face of the almost obtrusive use of two words in the original Greek. The rendering of the whole, however, is so inexact that it may be well to give it. Mrs. Lewis' translation is: "And when they had eaten, Jesus saith to Simon, Thou [art] Simon, son of Jonah, lovest thou me? He saith unto him, Yea, Lord. He saith unto him, Feed my lambs. Again Jesus saith to him, Thou [art] Simon, son of Jonah, lovest thou me much? He saith unto him, Yea, Lord. He saith unto him, Feed my sheep. Again Jesus saith unto him, Simon, son of Jonah, lovest thou me? Simon was grieved because three times Jesus spoke thus unto him. Simon saith unto him, Thou knowest all things; thou knowest that I love thee. And he said, Feed my flock." Here the word for love is found only four times, instead of the seven of the original, but the fourth time it is the rendering of φιλεῖς. Looking through the rest of John's Gospel, we find only four times in which another verb is used for love, אהב, just enough to show that the translator used רחם, not because there was absolutely no other, but because it was the regular, accepted word to denote love. Not only does he use it always to render φιλέω, except with the meaning to kiss, in all the Gospels, but thirty-six times for ἀγαπάω, as against eight times of אהב. In eighteen passages containing ἀγαπάω, and one containing φιλέω, the word is missing.

The Peshitto (perhaps A. D. 300) translates the dialogue much more literally than the Sinai MS., but gives seven times over the same רחם for love. Throughout the rest of the Gospel it follows the Old Syriac, in the main, for ἀγαπάω and φιλέω; two or three times deviating in favor of אחב for ἀγαπάω. In other parts of the New Testament, outside of Old Syriac influence, אחב is much more used, and exclusively in the epistles of John. Thus it seems that distinguishing between the two Greek originals was gaining ground, and in the Harklensian Version (A. D. 600), an extremely literal one, אחב, according to Bernstein, was uniformly used for ἀγαπάω, and רחם for φιλέω. The later versions, then, show a change under the pressure of the Greek, but leave unimpaired the testimony of Old Syriac to the older Aramaic. This testimony is corroborated by the Peshitto Old Testament, which, receiving no bias from its original, uniformly translates the Hebrew אהב by רחם.

But does not the fact that John uses so markedly the two words prove, against all other evidence, that two different words were employed in the conversation? It might possibly, if he were translating from a book, but not as reporting an interview. This brings us back to a characteristic of John's style, already noticed, viz., his duplicating Greek words. John was no master of Greek— he could write even πρῶτός μου ἦν (John i. 15, 30)—but he was a master of earnestness, and was willing to seek an elementary, not artistic, emphasis by varying and accumulating words whose differences he was not disposed to magnify. How far he was from critical precision in the use of ἀγαπάω and φιλέω he himself suggests by saying that Peter was grieved because Jesus said to him the third time φιλεῖς με; whereas in strict literalness he had said it but once. A good illustration of John's method is found in his use of two other words interwoven in this same passage with the words we are discussing—the threefold βόσκε . . . ποίμαινε . . . βόσκε. Here again the Old Syriac has but one word for "feed" —almost identical with the Hebrew רְעֵה—and the Peshitto version the same. John, however, interprets, and skillfully, the one Aramaic by the two Greek. It cannot be that he did not know and feel the difference between βόσκω and ποιμαίνω. We should have looked for but one Greek verb, the higher one, ποιμαίνω, as we find it from the lips of Paul in Acts xx. 28, "Feed the church of God," and in 1 Peter v. 2, but John combines the two. So we may say that he combines ἀγαπάω and φιλέω to bring out the whole of love. If he had been writing in Latin he would, doubtless, have used both *diligo* and *amo*, not to report a sort of word-play between Peter and his Master, but to say all that the Latin could say in unfolding love. If, however, he had been writing in English he would probably have been satisfied with the one word which, as in Hebrew and Aramaic, covers the whole field, and would hardly have placed in his margin: "The poverty of English prevents me from using two words for love instead of one."

The outcome of all this discussion is, that the New Testament writers, except John, followed the usage of the Septuagint, but with some religious momentum added to ἀγαπάω, as the word of the Divine Law "Thou shalt love," and of the worship of the Psalms. They recognized the lower plane of φιλέω, but John, in his Gospel, chose to put both words, for the time being, on a level, adding the warmth of one to the dignity of the other, that he might round out the expression of the enthusiasm of his life, the gospel of Divine Love.

VIII

THE HISTORICAL PRESENT IN THE FOUR GOSPELS

PROFESSOR BURTON in his "New Testament Moods and Tenses" gives the following definition of the historical present: "The Present Indicative is used to describe vividly a past event in the presence of which the speaker conceives himself to be." (§ 14.) But as the vividness admits of degrees, and sometimes lowers itself to a mere habit of style, we may say that every present that is used in narration where a past tense would be more exact, is a historical present. The Gospel of Mark, it is well known, contains many examples of this present. A class in New Testament Greek was once asked to compare the usage, in this respect, of the four Gospels by counting the examples in each. The result was as follows: Matthew 93, Mark 143, Luke 16, John 160. This should be modified, of course, by the fact that Mark is the shortest Gospel. If Mark be called 1, then John would be about 1¼, Matthew 1½, and Luke 1¾. Using this proportion, we correct the figures thus: Matthew 62, Mark 143, Luke 9, John 128. This represents the relative usage, and proves that, while there is a great difference between Mark and Matthew, and while Luke is almost out of consideration, there is practically no difference, in mere numbers, between Mark and John. In regard to the verbs that are used in the historical present, we should expect, in such narratives as the Gospels, a large use of "he says" and "he comes." Matthew uses λέγω 65 times, ἔρχομαι 5 times, and 15 other verbs together 23 times. Mark uses λέγω 68 times, ἔρχομαι 25 times, and 22 other verbs 50 times. Luke uses λέγω 9 times. John uses λέγω 117 times—λέγει 19 times in one chapter, the 21st, which is assumed to be genuine—ἔρχομαι 15 times, and 17 other verbs 28 times. The large number of different verbs indicates a fixed habit on the part of three of the Evangelists.

This usage forms a very simple, but trustworthy test of style and authorship. The test of vocabulary is less certain, because the acquisition of new words is more a matter of conscious purpose, and self-training, and is more dependent on circumstances, reading, and associates. A grammatical habit, though less obtrusive, is more fundamental, and a better sign of identity, because it is almost beneath consciousness. To affirm or deny authorship from vocabulary merely, is like judging handwriting by carefully formed capitals, instead of by the slope and angles and unintentional, almost unavoidable, peculiarities of the common letters.

A fine illustration of the historical present as a feature of style is furnished by Xenophon's Anabasis. Not only the ἐντεῦθεν ἐξελαύνει, of pleasant recollections, instead of ἤλασε (I. 2. 23), reiterates this tense, but the very first verb in the book is an historical present—Δαρείου καὶ Παρυσάτιδος γίγνονται παῖδες δύο—and that too with very little occasion for employing it. This lack of occasion indicates at the outset a *habit* of style. In the first three sections of Chapter I., containing only 16 Indicative tenses, and but little over 100 words (113), there are seven instances of the historical present, and 31 in the first two chapters. Thucydides has *one* (I. xxvi. 3) in the first 36 chapters of Book I.; but a fair comparison would make account of subject-matter.

The infrequency of this present in the Gospel of Luke raises the question whether it is found much in the Acts. If it were, one mark of Luke's authorship would be lacking. I have not been able to discover a single example, although many opportunities for its use occur, not only in general, but in the various riots described, and in the famous voyage and shipwreck. In regard to the differences between the first three Evangelists, they suggest that neither copied from the other; but each employed his own style on much common material, derived largely from Aramaic sources, either oral or written.

IX

DOES THE PREFACE TO LUKE'S GOSPEL BELONG ALSO TO THE ACTS?

Ἐπειδήπερ πολλοὶ ἐπεχείρησαν ἀνατάξασθαι διήγησιν περὶ τῶν πεπληροφορημένων ἐν ἡμῖν πραγμάτων, καθὼς παρέδοσαν ἡμῖν οἱ ἀπ᾽ ἀρχῆς αὐτόπται καὶ ὑπηρέται γενόμενοι τοῦ λόγου, ἔδοξε κἀμοὶ παρηκολουθηκότι ἄνωθεν πᾶσιν ἀκριβῶς καθεξῆς σοι γράψαι, κράτιστε Θεόφιλε, ἵνα ἐπιγνῷς περὶ ὧν κατηχήθης λόγων τὴν ἀσφάλειαν.

—Luke i. 1-4.

Τὸν μὲν πρῶτον λόγον ἐποιησάμην περὶ πάντων, ὦ Θεόφιλε, ὧν ἤρξατο ὁ Ἰησοῦς ποιεῖν τε καὶ διδάσκειν, ἄχρι ἧς ἡμέρας ἐντειλάμενος τοῖς ἀποστόλοις διὰ πνεύματος ἁγίου οὓς ἐξελέξατο ἀνελήμφθη.

—Acts i. 1, 2.

I ASSUME that Luke wrote both the Gospel that bears his name and the Acts. This, the traditional view, carrying with it the integrity, unity and trustworthiness of the Acts, is vigorously defended in Salmon's Introduction to the New Testament (1891), Lecture XVIII. Later, the same is maintained, from the standpoint of history and geography, by Professor Ramsay, against Spitta* and others, throughout his "St. Paul, the Traveller and the Roman Citizen" (1896). A new phase of the discussion was opened by Professor Fr. Blass,

---

*Die Apostelgeschichte, ihre Quellen und deren geschichtlicher Wert, von Friederich Spitta, 1891.

whose theory, briefly stated in the Prolegomena of his
"Acta Apostolorum, sive Lucae ad Theophilum Liber
Alter" (1895), pp. 30-32, is that Luke issued two editions
of the Acts, the first of which, afterwards revised by him
to our present text, is represented by the Codex Bezae.
This is supported by Otto Zöckler in Greifswalder
Studien (1895), pp. 109-145 (Die Apostelgeschichte als
Gegenstand höherer und niederer Kritik), and seems to
be endorsed by not a few scholars.

With these references to recent discussion, I take up
the question, "Does the Preface to Luke's Gospel belong
also to the Acts?" and remark—

1. That there is no express limitation confining the
coming narrative to the life of Christ. Such a limitation would be very natural, if it were intended to write
the Gospel only. The very language required may be
found in the first verse of the Acts; and we might expect Luke to write, "It seemed good to me also to relate
all that Jesus began both to do and teach, until the day in
which he was taken up." Such is not his statement.
Even the name of Jesus is not found. This cannot be
due to brevity, for the preface, though but a single sentence, is not concise, but somewhat ample in style. It
is true that if we take it for granted that it belongs to
the Gospel only, it is appropriate enough, but it is much
more appropriate if not confined to that. It is hardly
necessary to add that on this point no account should be
made of the order of the books in the Canon. The matter
should be viewed precisely as if the book of the Acts

followed immediately after the Gospel of Luke, with the intervention of no more than a few blank lines and a title. Doubtless Luke himself issued the two together after both had been written.

2. Some of the expressions in the preface foreshadow a longer period than is covered by the Gospel. The connected narrative ($\delta\iota\acute{\eta}\gamma\eta\sigma\iota\varsigma$) is to be (like that of "many"), "concerning those matters which have been fulfilled (Vulgate, completae sunt) among us." $\Pi\epsilon\pi\lambda\eta\rho o\phi o\rho\eta\mu\acute{\epsilon}\nu\omega\nu$ may mean "fully established" as an institution, or "fully proved." In either case Theophilus is to know the certainty of the instructions he has received; and Luke is to write "in order," because he has made careful investigation of "all things from the beginning ($\check{a}\nu\omega\theta\epsilon\nu$)." The promise, then, is to go over all the facts embraced in the Christian faith, and to confirm all the usual instructions given to converts. Could this promise be fulfilled without saying even a word about the outpouring of the Spirit at Pentecost? Would one writing more than twenty years after that Pentecost promise an account of all essential Christian facts, and yet not mean to say anything of those glorious years which were the crown and fulfillment of Christ's earthly life? Further, his promise is based on knowing "all things from the beginning." Does not this suggest that he will bring the history down from the beginning to about the time of writing? The moment we cease to take it for granted that this preface applies to the Gospel only, its expressions look towards a larger purpose. If there were no

subsequent book by the same writer, we could, indeed, interpret these expressions in a narrower sense, or, with Meyer, in a philosophical sense, as indicating that the gospel-history is the sure foundation of Christianity. But is it not better to say that the writer of these large promises, after fulfilling a part, laid down his pen for a short time, and then took it up again and fulfilled the rest?

One thing seems, at first view, to oppose what I have now urged. Luke appears to disclaim the character of eye-witness, and to depend for his authority on those who were "eye-witnesses and ministers of the word"; and yet in the latter part of the Acts he writes as an eye-witness of the life of Paul. In regard to this, these points should be noted: (1) The largest part of the Acts is as dependent on the testimony of others as the Gospel. (2) Even the original portions—the nine chapters at the close, and a part of the sixteenth—are largely made up of the testimony of Paul, a "minister of the word." (3) It would seem to be pressing the language unduly to insist that nothing whatever should be added from personal observation. (4) If the preface were written beforehand—and it may well have been—the author may not have known precisely at what point his narrative would stop.

3. The introduction to the Acts harmonizes with the idea that the book is a continuation originally intended, and not an afterthought. There is no proper preface, like that which is prefixed to the Gospel. There is

simply a statement of the ground already gone over in the Gospel, followed by a re-statement (verses 3-12), with additions, of the account of the parting words and the ascension, found in the closing verses of the Gospel. This is what we should expect if the Acts were Part II. of a continuous history. This impression is confirmed by the opening words, which refer to the Gospel as τὸν πρῶτον λόγον. The word λόγος itself favors this view somewhat, but is not decisive. Those who have not wholly forgotten their "Anabasis" will recall that in the opening sentence of each book after Book I., with a single exception, Xenophon gives a summary of the events gone over ἐν τῷ πρόσθεν λόγῳ. The λόγος referred to in the opening of the second book is Book I. In the other cases it means the narrative contained in all the preceding books; but in no case does it designate a work other than the Anabasis. So Herodotus in his second book (38) says of matters afterwards mentioned in Book III., τὰ ἐγὼ ἐν ἄλλῳ λόγῳ ἐρέω; and in referring (V. 36) to certain offerings of Crœsus mentioned in Book I. 92, he says, ὡς δεδήλωταί μοι ἐν τῷ πρώτῳ τῶν λόγων. Here the usage is just like that of the Latin *liber*. There seems to be no such usage in the New Testament, unless this in the Acts be a case of it. In Greek of the times, outside of the New Testament, the usage is not unknown, as is shown by Birt in "Das antike Buchwesen" (p. 28). In titles, which, though not to be depended on as of the same age as their books, may yet have some value for traditional usage, we find that Josephus has λόγος in the Jewish War, though βίβλος in the Antiquities; Dionysius Hal. has λόγος, also Philo in the Life of Moses, and Lucian.

But without making too much of λόγος, we may say that the phrase τὸν πρῶτον λόγον seems like the numbering of distinct portions of a work. Professor Ramsay argues (St. Paul, etc., p. 28) that the phrase "is more reconcilable with the plan of three books than of two." In Lucian's True History, however, (perhaps A. D. 150) we find, as title, Ἀληθοῦς Ἱστορίας λόγος πρῶτος, although there are but two books. The entire impression seems to me to be that this second λόγος is not an independent διήγησις, but Part II. of the διήγησις promised in the preface.

4. It is generally agreed that Luke did actually write the Acts shortly after the Gospel. It is therefore very improbable that he did not have in mind doing so when he began the Gospel. Is it not, indeed, likely that his familiarity with the later events led him to follow back to its sources (παρακολουθεῖν) the whole history? Thus the Acts, while yet unwritten, would give rise to the Gospel. Alford thinks (Proleg. Luke, sec. iv.) that at least five years intervened between the publication of the Gospel and the Acts; and his principal reason is that the account of the ascension is much fuller in the latter, indicating access to additional information. But how long can we assume that it would take a historian to get new information? It might be five years or five days. A very diligent and careful investigator, like Luke,

would be quite as likely to find it soon as late. We can see no good ground for questioning the common opinion that the Gospel was written but a short time before the Acts; say, during the two years of Paul's first imprisonment. If this is so, the preface can hardly be divorced from the Acts.

The evidence, then, seems to show that while the preface to the Gospel is not such a one as would be written after both works were completed, yet it was written with both in mind. Whatever may have been the interval of publication, the whole work might be entitled, The history of the establishment of the Christian faith. —Part I. The life of Jesus; Part II. The manifestation of the Holy Spirit, and the founding of the church.

X

CHRIST'S DESCENT INTO HADES

Οὐκ ἐγκαταλείψεις τὴν ψυχήν μου εἰς ᾅδην. Acts ii. 27 (Ps. xvi. 10).

Ἀναβὰς εἰς ὕψος ᾐχμαλώτευσεν αἰχμαλωσίαν. Eph. iv. 8.

"HE descended into hell"—so runs the venerable and majestic Creed. But the American Episcopal Prayer-book prefixes its timid rubric as follows: "Any churches may omit the words 'He descended into hell,' or may, instead of them, use the words 'He went into the place of departed spirits,' which are considered as words of the same meaning in the Creed." The words which are here made optional have come down to us in an unbroken line of doctrinal succession from the fourth century. They have, indeed, been stigmatized as an interpolation, but so early an interpolation might perhaps be called a mature addition. Their omission in English was favored by the change of meaning in the word "hell," but there was also the feeling that Christ's visit to Hades was of little importance, and is to us not a doctrine, but a matter of mere curiosity.

Now, whatever may be true of the "Apostles' Creed," the Descent into Hades has a sufficient New Testament authority. The first recorded address of Peter contains twofold evidence that the Descent was believed by both speaker and hearers. In the first place, he quotes from a Psalm (xvi.) that had a shaping influence on the belief of the people respecting Hades. Further, he bases an argument and appeal for the resurrection of Christ on the certainty that he would not stay in Hades. "Thou wilt not leave my soul in Hades."

But what was Hades, and what the significance and importance of Christ's going thither? In a somewhat recent discussion I find these words: "The Savior was in the same state between death and resurrection as we now are after death." This is, it seems to me, precisely what ought *not* to be said. For this ignores the whole work of Christ in Hades, and leaves them that sleep in Jesus no better off than if he had not risen. Let us put ourselves in the place of the apostles and their fellow disciples, and after we have learned the truth about Hades as it appeared in their thought and forms of statement, then we may, if we can, translate it into our own thoughts and forms of statement. Hades was the region where dwelt the souls that were under the power of death. The souls of the righteous as well as of the wicked were under this awful power. Into this region came the soul of the Crucified, but it did not remain there. Going thither was the lowest point in his humiliation, and leaving was the beginning of his triumph. What, then, was the effect *in Hades* of this visit and this departure? But this is the same as to ask, What was the effect, in the spirit-world, of the resurrection? According to the apocryphal Gospel of Nicodemus, or Acts of

Pilate,—of perhaps the fourth century,—two of the saints that arose at the resurrection of Christ, Charinus and Lenthius, sons of Simeon, wrote out all that they were allowed to reveal of the coming of Jesus into Hades. This Gospel was the basis of the mediæval miracle play "The Harrowing of Hell." The work in Hades, here somewhat grotesquely described, was the deliverance from hell of the ancient saints, and may be summed up in a single one of its own sentences—"And taking hold of Adam by his right hand, he ascended from hell, and all the saints of God followed him."*

I do not say that the Gospel of Nicodemus is to be trusted, but it may be as near the truth as the statement that "the Savior was in the same state between death and the resurrection as we now are after death"—a statement that would be accepted, probably, by a majority of Christians. A dear friend writes me, "I have no prejudice against Hades, and when I die, I expect to go there"; but surely he is not thinking of the Hades in the minds of the apostles and primitive disciples. After they had come to understand the resurrection of Christ and feel its power, they were filled with what may be called the resurrection-enthusiasm. In their view the resurrection-era was already begun. Death and hell [Hades] were vanquished. Wesley's hymn has the true apostolic spirit:—

> "Our Lord is risen from the dead,
> Our Jesus is gone up on high;
> The powers of hell are captive led,
> Dragged to the portals of the sky."

---
*Gospel of Nicodemus, xix. 12

Just when the resurrection was to take visible effect in themselves, the disciples could not say, and it did not matter. To die was to go and be with him who had risen. And such a dying did not deserve the name of death. It was a sleep; it was the putting off of this tabernacle; it was a departure; it was not the death that all past ages had known, for Jesus had said: "He that liveth and believeth in me shall never die."

To the question why the *Descensus* is not oftener spoken of in the New Testament, the answer is, that going to Hades is taken for granted as a part of death. It was not necessary to speak of both whenever either was mentioned. In the Revelation, indeed, the two are linked together: "I have the keys of death and of Hades" (i. 18); "His name was death, and Hades followed with him" (vi. 8); "And death and Hades gave up the dead which were in them. . . . And death and Hades were cast into the lake of fire" (xx. 13, 14). The mention of either was logically sufficient. Ἅιδης, both in heathen and Biblical usage, represents death in its relation to the soul. But the Hades of the Bible is not a home for believers, even temporarily. It is Hades triumphed over by him who "brought life and incorruption [exemption from death] to light." "When he ascended on high he led captivity captive" (Eph. iv. 8). Death was "swallowed up in victory" (1 Cor. xv. 54). The resurrection-enthusiasm of the New Testament is the response of faith to those glorious words, "I go to prepare a place for you," which place was not in Hades. The same divine enthusiasm refused to recognize any "intermediate state," the old abolished Hades under a new name. Stephen did not say, "Behold, I see the Son of man in Hades." Can we wonder that the early disciples looked for a speedy return of the Lord? Does one say, It was an error? It was not; for it was necessary to the highest truth. The resurrection-spirit refused to see the long interval of waiting. As has been said of the prophets that they looked from one mountain-top of history to another, and could not see the low-lying valleys between, so we may say of the apostles, that they saw the triumph over death and hell as a complete victory, and they would have been false to the *power* of the truth, if they had not looked upon it as gloriously near. "The reign of Death is over; Hades is abolished; Life and Immortality have come"—this is the key-note of the resurrection-spirit. Christ's resurrection might as well be called a resurrection from Hades as from the grave.

I will not dwell on the preaching to "the spirits in prison" (1 Pet. iii. 18-20). It cannot be needful that there should be a thousand and one expositions of that passage, instead of simply a thousand; but the point of view we are taking has to do with it in at least two particulars:—

1. The Descent was necessary without any regard to the preaching. The Descent itself, however, was a proclamation of unspeakable meaning. The inhabitants of the spirit-world were not in solitary confinement or unconscious sleep. They saw the Redeemer at the lowest

point in his work of redemption, and at the beginning of his triumph.

2. This preaching looks backward to the past. This is in harmony with the idea that Hades was now abolished, and the spirit-world revolutionized. We might *imagine* that the object of the Descent was to plant the Christian church in Hades and ordain for it a succession of Hades-apostles, and so forth, but the view of Peter was that Hades came to an end. The preaching was once for all. Why the antediluvians are referred to may perhaps be explained by the fact that so vast a number, going to their death in an awful catastrophe, made them the representatives and types of the Hades-world. It might have given the name of Antediluvian under-world. If one asks, Why should not those who have since died hear the preaching also? the Scripture gives no answer. A perpetual Hades with perpetual preaching in it is nowhere revealed.

In regard to the whole question of the relation of the wicked to the resurrection, we need not wonder at the infrequent allusions to the risen wicked. The epistles of the New Testament are addressed to Christians. Paul's great argument in 1 Cor. xv. runs into a grand anthem of Christian triumph. We cannot suppose that the enthusiasm of the apostles would rise over the fate of the wicked as over the redemption of the saints. But the resurrection-influence certainly reaches the wicked. One saying of the Master settles that: "They that have done good unto the resurrection of life; and they that have done ill unto the resurrection of judgment" (John v. 29). This did not need for its certainty the echo of Paul: "There shall be a resurrection both of the just and unjust" (Acts xxiv. 15). The judgment scene in Matt. xxv. implies the resurrection of the wicked. The resurrection period ends with the judgment. The divine foreshortening places the coming in glory close by the resurrection. But we have the right to follow apostolic example, and avert our eyes from the fate of the wicked, and rejoice in the glory of the redeemed.

Christ's Descent, or rather Ascent, opened the resurrection-era in the spirit-world as well as on earth, and began the fulfillment of the promise, "I go to prepare a place for you." Shall we translate the apostolic thoughts and visions into modern thoughts and views? We cannot expect to comprehend fully the results of Christ's death and resurrection in the unseen world. That it was a revolution is the unspoken testimony of our hearts whenever we think of those dear to us who sleep in Jesus, and whenever we look forward to our own death, which Hope names a resurrection-sleep. We are still living in the resurrection-era. When we die we shall not pass beyond the resurrection-influence. How shall we express this hope and faith? Shall we say, in the words of the shorter Westminster, "The souls of believers are at their death made perfect in holiness, and do immediately pass into glory"? But to show the very heart and substance of the doctrine of Christ's Descent into Hades—its depth of humiliation, its triumph, and its glorious fruits—the Te Deum is better than the Catechism:—

"When thou had'st overcome the sharpness of death,
Thou did'st open the kingdom of heaven to all believers."

XI

APPOINTED TO ETERNAL LIFE

'Επίστευσαν ὅσοι ἦσαν τεταγμένοι εἰς ζωὴν αἰώνιον. Acts xiii. 48.

Τάσσω is a word of order, arrangement. Soldiers in array are τεταγμένοι, each in his place. Those new Gentile converts were not acting at haphazard, when they were so ready to believe, but each in accordance with his history and character, and with the Divine arrangement of his life. This appointing to eternal life is called by our Savior "giving." In words of great tenderness he says, "All that which the Father giveth me shall come unto me, and him that cometh to me I will in no wise cast out" (John vi. 37). It also goes by the names "calling," "choice," "election," but perhaps no word comes so well into line with modern thought as τεταγμένος, which links the present and future to the past and to the throne of God. Such appointment, or election, is not restriction, but rather extension. The tone of the statement is comprehensive, not exclusive. We must not begin it "Only as many as," "The few that," but "All that." This the Greek ὅσοι requires. These Gentiles of Antioch were a notable accession to the infant Church. Divine election broadens, not narrows, the field of Christianity. It secures, not obstructs salvation.

The linking of eternal life to God's purpose and man's

faith has a very definite relation to the dogma, or hope, of probation beyond the grave. Those who are appointed to eternal life will not fail of it. This settles the question of future probation by destroying interest in it. Probation is not fundamental, but faith is. The smallest germ of faith secures salvation, with or without probation. Probation, or rather the gospel, develops that germ, fills the believing with a new life, and gives the world a present salvation, but is not needed in order to reveal any man's character to God. The number of the saved includes all in whom God's eye detects faith, whether developed or not.

XII

AGRIPPA TO PAUL: ACTS XXVI. 28, IN THE LIGHT OF
LATIN IDIOM

The influence of Latin on the Greek of New Testament times is unquestioned. Not only single Latin words, as κεντυρίων, are found in the New Testament, but translated phrases, as ἐργασίαν δοῦναι (*operam dare*). The influence of Latin idiom would naturally be looked for in a report of the language of one brought up at Rome and speaking Greek before a Roman tribunal. Such a report we have in these words (according to the best text), Ἐν ὀλίγῳ με πείθεις Χριστιανὸν ποιῆσαι. This is translated in the Revised Version: "With but little persuasion thou wouldst fain make me a Christian." This is certainly ingenious, but is it not forced? Why cannot Χριστιανὸν ποιῆσαι mean "to act the part of a Christian"? The Latin *agere* furnishes numerous parallels in writers of the Silver Age. According to Tacitus, Piso says of Otho that his vices ruined the government, *etiam cum amicum imperatoris ageret*, "even when he was acting the part of a friend of the emperor." Hist. 1.30. Mucianus is said to be *socium magis imperii quam ministrum agens*, "acting as an ally rather than a servant of the government." Hist. 2.83. Thrasea is said *agere senatorem*, "to act the senator." Annals 16.28. Quintilian says of Socrates, *Agens imperitum et admiratorem aliorum tanquam sapientium*, "acting the part of an ignoramus and an admirer of others as if they were wise." Inst. Or. 9. 2. 46. Also 11. 3. 91. and 12. 8. 10. The following examples are found in the Letters of Pliny: *Sunt qui defunctorum quoque amicos agant*, "act the part of friends." I. 17. 1. *Amissoque filio matrem adhuc agere*, "though the son was lost still to play the mother." III. 16. 6. *Patrem familiae hactenus ago*, "I play the householder." ix. 15. 3. Pliny's Panegyric has these two: *Tunc maxime imperator cum amicum ex imperatore agis*. 85. 6. *Cum agere tam bonum consulem posses.* 56. 3. A tragedy of Seneca, a contemporary of Paul, has the following line (Clytaemnestra to Electra): *Sed agere domita feminam disces malo*, "Tamed by misfortune, thou shalt learn to play the woman." Agam. v. 3. 7. Suetonius has several examples: *Non principem sed ministrum egit*. Claud. 29. Also Tiber. 12. 26. Valerius Maximus, writing in the reign of Tiberius, gives us at least twelve instances of this usage. Speaking of the first Brutus, and of the execution of his sons, he says, *Exuit patrem ut consulem ageret*. v. 8. 1. Of the famous Scaevola and his recreations he says, *Ut enim in rebus seriis Scaevolam, ita et in* [scenicis] *lusibus hominem agebat*. viii. 8. 2. In the same way *agere* is used with *amicum* iv. 2. 5., *consulem* ii. 2. 4., iii. 8. 3., 12. 2. 2., *feneratricem* viii. 2. 2., *virum, imperatorem* vii. 2. 5., *maritum, patrem* ix. 13. 4., *praetorem*, vii. 7. 7., *custodem* vi. 1. 4., *reum, accusatorem* iv. 2. 6., *civem* viii. 6. 2. Velleius Paterculus, also in the time of Tiberius, has *agebat aemulum*, Maroboduus "was playing the rival," 11. 109. 1. He says of Tiberius that he was striving *ut potius aequalem civem quam eminentem liceret agere principem*. 11. 124. 2 . Also 11. 92. 2. The fact that these examples are from the later Latin will not detract from their value. The distinction between *agere* and *facere* is not important in the idiom. We may add a single example of *facere* from Plautus, *Ferocem facis*, "you put on a bold face, *lit.* do the bold man." Most. iv. i. 32 (44).

If this idiom be disallowed, it is still possible to derive a similar meaning by taking Χριστιανὸν as neuter, though we should expect the plural, as in Herodotus v. 40, ποιέων οὐδαμῶς Σπαρτιητικά. In either case, the unusual meaning of ποιῆσαι may possibly explain the early change of the text to γενέσθαι (from Paul's answer), from which comes our received rendering, "thou persuadest me to *be* a Christian."

The meaning "act the part of" would receive support, independently of the Latin, from one passage in the Septuagint, if the text were undisputed. In 1 Kings (3 Reg.) xx. (xxi.) 7, Jezebel says to Ahab, Σὺ νῦν οὕτω ποιεῖς βασιλέα ἐπὶ 'Ισραήλ; "Art thou thus acting the king over Israel?" But a variant for βασιλέα is βασιλείαν, which indeed our Hebrew text would require.

Unless Χριστιανὸν ποιῆσαι be taken to mean "to act the Christian" we seem to be driven to a very awkward connection of ποιῆσαι with πείθεις. Πείθω needs a personal subject for a dependent infinitive. "You are persuading me to do" something, is intelligible and natural, but how about "You are persuading to make me"? It can hardly mean "You are trying by persuasion to make me" or "You are prevailing to make me," i. e., succeeding in making; nor do I see how it can mean "You would fain make me." Besides, the position of με in the sentence is against its being the object of ποιῆσαι. Would it not in that case be nearer ποιῆσαι? The latest eminent commentator on Acts, Professor Blass, following Codex Alexandrinus, adopts into his text πείθῃ, saying in emphatic Latin, "πείθεις . . . ποιῆσαι ferri nequit." His rendering is: "Brevi tempore tibi persuades te Christianum me reddidisse."

Is there not also a Latin idiom in ἐν ὀλίγῳ? Readers of Livy find numerous examples of *in* with the ablative, forming phrases equivalent to adjectives and adverbs; as *in propinquo*, *in promiscuo*, *in facili*, *in difficili*, etc. There may be no literary examples of *in parvo*, or *in paulo*, but we have *in angusto* (=*angustus*, Celsus, De Med. 8. 4, twice), and Tacitus, speaking of the dreary monotony of cruelty in his history, says "Nobis *in arto* et inglorius labor." Ann. 4. 32. 3. So we have in our day the traditional phrases *in toto*, *in extenso*. It can hardly be claimed that ἐν ὀλίγῳ is a borrowed phrase, but it may possibly have an adverbial force, determined by Latin idiom. It would then be not the same as ἐν ὀλίγῳ in Eph. iii. 3, "in brief" ("as I wrote afore in few words"), but like ὀλίγως in 2 Peter ii. 18 —τοὺς ὀλίγως ἀποφεύγοντας, "those that are escaping a *little*." Then the whole passage would read, somewhat literally: "Agrippa said unto Paul, A little thou art persuading me to act the Christian. And Paul said, I would to God, that both a little and a great deal, not thou only, but also all that hear me this day, might become such as I am, except these bonds."

XIII

RECONCILIATION BY SELF-REVELATION

Δικαιούμενοι δωρεὰν τῇ αὐτοῦ χάριτι διὰ τῆς ἀπολυτρώσεως τῆς ἐν Χριστῷ Ἰησοῦ, ὃν προέθετο ὁ Θεὸς ἱλαστήριον διὰ πίστεως ἐν τῷ αὐτοῦ αἵματι, εἰς ἔνδειξιν τῆς δικαιοσύνης αὐτοῦ. Rom. iii. 24, 25.

THE Revised Version of verses 24-26 is as follows: "Being justified freely by his grace through the redemption that is in Christ Jesus: whom God set forth to be a propitiation, through faith, by his blood, to show his righteousness, because of the passing over of the sins done aforetime, in the forbearance of God; for the showing, I say, of his righteousness at this present season: that he might himself be just, and the justifier of him that hath faith in Jesus." If there is any passage in the New Testament that contains the philosophy of the atonement in its relation to justice, it is this; but that philosophy is here only incidental, and is discovered not by hair-splitting discussions of δικαιόω, ἀπολύτρωσις, and ἱλαστήριον, but by observing the antithesis between justice and forgiveness as overcome by God's manifestation of himself; an antithesis not obtruded, but involved in the contrast between law and grace. Throughout the whole passage there is an undertone of unwillingness to forgive without doing something in the interest of righteousness, something to prevent the lowering of its supremacy; but there is implied no unwillingness to do that something. Much has been said of the dishonor done to God by supposing him unwilling to forgive sin. All theology has echoed with the cry: "Down with the thought that God needs to be made willing to forgive!" But how about the thought that God makes himself willing, or rather is eternally willing to forgive in his own way of attendant self-manifestation? No doubt there has been in common theories a false antithesis between the Divine attributes of justice and love, as if they belonged to different beings. There is indeed a difference in the Divine attitude towards good and towards evil that needs strong emphasis—towards sin the Divine frown and wrath, and zeal for its overwhelming and everlasting overthrow, towards righteousness the Divine smile and joy and infinite zeal for its enthronement. But that zeal that burns with so hot a flame against sin, and glows so brightly for righteousness,—when it meets human life, is so interfused with yearning to save the lost that it seems but another name for love. There has been also a false antithesis between justice and love, as to their attracting and transforming power. Righteousness draws, and holiness draws, as well as love and mercy.

Now God's revelation of himself is a true and perfect satisfaction of justice, even, if you please, of *retributive* justice, because it accomplishes abundantly the ends of retribution by enthroning right and dethroning wrong more completely than could punishment, be it ever so severe, be it universal and eternal. Is this a philosophy of the atonement? Not exactly, but a broad and deep foundation for it. "In respect to the propitiatory efficacy of the atonement, pardon is dependent not on penal satisfaction, nor on mere sustained authority, but on the satisfaction of self-revelation, or such a complete exhibition of God's righteous character as forever settles the question of his essential and eternal justice. The atonement embodies this justice in a living Example, and thus makes it a restoring power in humanity."*

---

*This quotation is from an article entitled "The Atonement as a Revelation," published in the New Englander for April, 1864. Compare also an article, "The Atonement in the Light of Conscience," in the Bibliotheca Sacra for January, 1867.

XIV

THE MEANING OF "FOREKNEW" IN ROMANS VIII. 29, AS ILLUSTRATED BY JOHN X. 27

IN English usage we do not speak of foreknowing a *person*. In fact we use the word seldom even with an impersonal object, preferring "foresee"; as, "He foresaw the result," "He foresaw the man in the child." But our usage is different from that of the New Testament. Not except in a translation should we write such a sentence as this: "God hath not cast away his people which he *foreknew*" (Rom. xi. 2). The Latin usage resembles the English. The Greek itself is without usage, so far as I can find, outside of the New Testament, in connecting the compound προγιγνώσκω with a personal object. In the Septuagint the word occurs but three times (in the Apocrypha, Sap. vi. 13; viii. 9; xviii. 6), and with an impersonal object.

This state of the case plainly directs us to consult the usage of the uncompounded verb. Even here classical Greek gives little help; but we get some light from the Old Testament and the Hebrew יָדַע (LXX. γινώσκω). This word, which, like all the other Hebrew verbs, admits no prepositions in composition, has a very wide meaning; and there are two or three examples that remind one of the passage in Romans. "The Lord . . . *knoweth* them that put their trust in him" (Nah. i . 7); "You only have I *known* of all the families of the earth" (Amos iii. 2).

But the clearest light comes from the New Testament itself, and especially from the tenth chapter of John. For comparison let us take Rom. viii. 29, 30, 35, 38, 39: "For whom he foreknew, he also foreordained to be conformed to the image of his Son, that he might be the first-born among many brethren; and whom he foreordained, them he also called; and whom he called, them he also justified; and whom he justified, them he also glorified. . . . Who shall separate us from the love of Christ? . . . For I am persuaded that neither death, nor life, nor angels, nor principalities, nor things present, nor things to come, nor powers, nor height, nor depth, nor any other creature, shall be able to separate us from the love of God, which is in Christ Jesus our Lord." Then John x. 27, 28, 16: "My sheep hear my voice, and I know them, and they follow me: and I give unto them eternal life; and they shall never perish, and no one shall snatch them out of my hand." "And other sheep I have which are not of this fold: them also I must bring, and they shall hear my voice."

The comparison between these passages should apply not to a single word merely, but to the course of thought. In Romans the order is (1) foreknowing, (2) foreordaining, (3) calling, (4) a sure and glorious salvation. In John it is (1) the call, (2) the hearing and coming, (3) the recognition and following, (4) a sure eternal life.

My voice they hear, I know them, they follow me, I give them eternal life. In John, also, we have the thought, without the word "*fore*know." The Shepherd's eye is on "other sheep which are not of this fold," *future* instead of *present* disciples. He foreknows them. He must bring them and they shall hear his voice; i. e., whom he foreknows he also calls. Our Lord says nothing here of foreordaining, but the thought is close by (verse 29): "My Father which *hath given them unto me* is greater than all, and no man is able to snatch them out of the Father's hand,"—quite parallel with those other words (vi. 37): "All that which the Father giveth me shall come unto me, and him that cometh unto me I will in no wise cast out."

Such a comparison as I have only outlined, strengthens the first impression, that what "know" means in John, "foreknow" means in Romans, with the addition of "beforehand." And "I know them," in John means, obviously, "I recognize them as my own." Christ knows his own, as a shepherd knows every one of his sheep, as a mother knows her child, as brother knows brother, and friend friend.

Is this foreknowing the same as foreordination? The answer from John is in the negative; for, besides the knowing, there is the giving by the Father. And such is the natural impression of Paul's own words. "Foreknew" is the first link in the chain that ends with "glorified."

Is foreknowing the same as election? That depends on

what election is. It is not the same, if election is a part of foreordination. But if election means fixing the eye of recognition and love on each disciple, present or future, then this knowing, or foreknowing, is election.

I am not discussing the use of γινώσκω in general in the New Testament. I will cite only two other passages: those judgment-words, "I never *knew* you" (Matt. vii. 23), where the meaning seems precisely the same as in John x. 27, and "The Lord *knoweth* them that are his" (2 Tim. ii. 19),—from the Septuagint of Num. xvi. 5—where the meaning is substantially the same.

In Romans xi. 2—"God hath not cast away his people which he *foreknew*,"—the prefix "fore" seems to denote not "looking into the future," but simply "before now," the writer looking back into the past. "God hath not cast off his people which in time past, ever of old, he recognized as his own." He is unchangeable, and his past choice and purpose shall stand.

XV

PAUL'S ANATHEMA

Ηὐχόμην γὰρ ἀνάθεμα εἶναι αὐτὸς ἐγὼ ἀπὸ τοῦ Χριστοῦ. Rom. ix. 3.

THE right explanation of Rom. ix. 3 illustrates more than one important principle of exegesis. One is this: *Theological inferences are of no account against the simple, obvious meaning of a passage.* The theological pressure on this passage is well expressed in the Bibliotheca Sacra for July, 1894: "The usual exegesis makes Paul willing to be excluded from all hope of salvation, including not only endless suffering, but also positive enmity toward Christ forever" (p. 512). This consideration is made to support the rendering, "For I myself did wish to be separated from Christ," the reference being to Paul's life before conversion.

Now against this pressure from without is the fact that the passage itself, if translated "I wished," etc., is not a natural reference to Paul's past life. He refers to that life more than once with a definiteness and warmth that leave no doubt as to his meaning. He could say, "I verily thought with myself that I ought to do many things contrary to the name of Jesus of Nazareth. . . . Being exceedingly mad against them, I persecuted them" (Acts xxvi.9,11). "Beyond measure I persecuted the church of God, and made havoc of it" (Gal. 1. 13). He could humble himself to say "that am not meet to be called an apostle, because I persecuted the church of God" (1 Cor. xv. 9). It is incredible that such a bare, uncircumstantial statement as is proposed, should be Paul's confession as a persecutor. The obvious impression is against it. No one would think of it except under outside doctrinal pressure. And for this obvious impression there are at least two distinct reasons: 1. The expression "anathema *from* Christ" is appropriate only in the mouth of a Christian, or one who considers himself a Christian. It implies renunciation of Christ and banishment from him. 2. The clause contains no adverb of past time which would make it read thus, "I myself *once* [ποτέ] wished." "But," one may say, "take heed to your grammar, and obey the imperfect tense, with or without ποτέ." Here appears a second rule of exegesis: *Avoid what may be called a mechanical use of grammar.* A sentence is not a piece of dead mechanism, grinding out its meaning by the levers and wheels of mood and tense; it participates in the life and flexibility and sensitiveness of the mind that produces it. Grammar is corrective, not creative; a good servant, but a bad master. Formal grammar is ultimately derived from the meaning, and not the meaning from grammar.

All that has now been said implies, or half implies, that the theological pressure on this passage is valid and weighty; but it is not. If it were, it would be one's duty to resist it, but there is really nothing to resist. By a cool analysis some of us have found dreadful things in the passage, but cool analysis is here out of place. The words are a hot outburst of devotion and love. "Let Paul go down—down to everlasting destruction, if only Israel may be lifted up to salvation." The apostle did not stop to measure his words, and we shall get his meaning not by picking away at the syllables, but by catching the spirit and feeling. "Was Paul then a Hopkinsian, 'willing to be damned'? Was he willing to be an enemy of Christ? Willing to sin forever?" No; if you speak of deliberate choice. But he was not expressing deliberate choice, but the most undeliberate passion of love. The language of logic failed him, and the language of pain and agony took its place. "Did he, then, mean what he said?" Rather he meant what he *felt*. He did not mean all that we can possibly find in his words. He uncovered his throbbing heart; that was all, that was enough—too much for modern cool-headed analysis. We, then, see illustrated a third rule of exegesis, which may, perhaps, be expressed thus: *When a writer does not measure his words, the reader should not.*

XVI

WORDS BORROWED FROM THE LATIN

'Ην γεγραμένον 'Εβραιστί, 'Ρωμαιστί, 'Ελληνιστί. John xix. 20.

The following words are borrowed from the Latin:—
'Ασσάριον. This was the only Greek word for the Latin *as;* the nearest coin-word in genuine Greek being ὀβολός. It is generally explained as a diminutive, with the suffix *-αριον*. If the *a* of its second syllable could be proved short, this origin would be indisputable. In Smith's Dictionary of Classical Antiquities the word is identified with an old doublet of *as*, viz., *assarius*. This seems the more probable origin, the neuter being used as in δηνάριον, because νόμισμα takes the place of *nummus*. Certainly the two sigmas seem borrowed from the Latin, in which the *s* was regularly doubled, as in the case-forms of *as*, the verb *esse*, etc., to prevent the lapse to *r*. I see no reason in Greek phonology why the word should not have been ἀσάριον, if it is a hybrid diminutive. But aside from this, the earliest appearance in literature of ἀσσάριον suggests the very opposite of *little as*. Dionysius Hal. (B. C. 30) says (Antiq. Rom. 9. 27) that Menenius Agrippa, the Younger, was fined 2,000 ἀσσάρια, and adds ἦν δ' ἀσσάριον χάλκεον νόμισμα, βάρος λιτριαῖον, i. e., the *as libralis*, the "pound as." the

earliest and heaviest. Plutarch says (Camillus 13) that Camillus was fined 15,000 ἀσσάρια, which he explains as equal to 1,500 drachmæ; and Livy in stating the same fact (v. 32), gives the same amount in *aes grave* (=*as libralis*). Plutarch also uses the word in describing the home life of the elder Cato. Since both these writers were narrating ancient history, the old name *assarius* might have been found in their Latin authorities. Indeed, though used but little in extant Latin, it occurs in one of the grammatical discussions of Varro (L. L. 8. 71), who was almost a contemporary of Dionysius. A century earlier Polybius speaks of the ἡμιασσάριον as a common price for entertainment at an inn, reminding one of the δύο δηνάρια of the Good Samaritan. It may be added that no reason is apparent for a diminutive meaning. If it had been of silver, like the Roman *libella*, which was an *as* in value, but only 1-16 of its size, we should have a reason, but it was undoubtedly a copper coin; and though it had received at different times great reductions, yet, as I have said, ἀσσάριον was the only word used for whatever period. I have been unable to find an example, outside of the New Testament, where it was connected with current events. The *as* in New Testament times was worth about 8 mills of our money. The English "happeny" would more nearly represent it than the "farthing" with which we now associate the sale of the sparrows. Matt. x. 29. Luke xii. 6.

Δηνάριον, Latin *denarius*, classical Greek δραχμή. This was equal to ten *asses* (*deni asses*), or sixteen cents before the *as* was reduced to its lowest value. In New Testament times it was equal to sixteen *asses*, or about thirteen cents. Thus the translation "six-pence" would be more nearly correct than "penny." The denarius (from which comes the "d," for pence, of English sterling currency) was a silver coin, bearing on one side the image of the emperor. Hence the question of Jesus, "Whose image," etc. The pay of the common Roman soldier was ten *asses* a day after the *as* was reduced. At the accession of Tiberius (A. D. 14) the soldiers in Pannonia revolted, and, among other complaints, they said that "soul and body were estimated at ten asses a day," and that out of this clothes, arms, tents, etc., had to be purchased. Their demand was, that "their daily wages should be a *denarius*" (i. e., a sixteen-as denarius), although the prætorian cohorts, or imperial guards, received *two* denarii.* This will illustrate the wages in the parable of the vineyard. A penny, or six-pence, a day was enough for a full day's work, and a generous gratuity for the last hour's work. The word is found sixteen times in the New Testament. The unmerciful servant found one "which owed him an hundred *pence*," Matt. xviii. 28. The householder "agreed with the laborers for a *penny* a day," Matt. xx. 2, 9, 10, 13. The Hero-

---

*Enimvero militiam ipsam gravem, infructuosam: *denis* in diem *assibus* animam et corpus aestimari: hinc vestem, arma, tentoria, hinc saevitiam centurionum et vacationes munerum redimi. At hercule verbera et vulnera, duram hiemem, exercitas aestates, bellum atrox aut sterilem pacem sempiterna. Nec aliud levamentum quam si certis sub legibus militia iniretur, ut *singulos denarios* mererent, sextus decimus stipendii annus finem afferret, ne ultra sub vexillis tenerentur, sed iisdem in castris praemium pecunia solveretur. An praetorias cohortes, quae *binos denarios* acciperent, quae post sedecim annos penatibus suis reddantur, plus periculorum suscipere?—Tacitus, Annals, i. 17. Ut denarius diurnum stipendium foret. i. 26.

dians "brought unto him a *penny*," Matt. xxii. 19; Mark xii. 15; Luke xx. 24. The disciples in the desert-place asked, "Shall we go and buy two hundred *penny*worth of bread?" Mark vi. 37; John vi. 7. The ointment of spikenard "might have been sold for more than three hundred *pence*," Mark xiv. 5; John xii. 5. One of the two debtors "owed five hundred *pence*," Luke vii. 41. The good Samaritan "took out two *pence*," Luke x. 35. A voice in Revelation said, "A measure of wheat for a *penny*, and three measures of barley for a *penny*." Rev. vi. 6. Plutarch uses δηνάριον, δραχμή, and δεκάχαλκον.

Κεντυρίων—Latin *centurio*, from *centuria* (*centum-vir*), a commander of a hundred men, a captain. The regular Greek word is ἑκατοντάρχης or ἑκατόνταρχος, which latter word is generally used in the New Testament. Mark uses κεντυρίων. At the crucifixion we read of "the *centurion*, which stood over against him," Mark xv. 39; also verses 44, 45. The word is found in Polybius.

Κῆνσος—Latin *census*, originally the property-list of the Roman people, from *censere*, to rate; φόρος would be the regular Greek word. The examples of its use are, "What thinkest thou, Simon? of whom do the kings of the earth take custom or *tribute?*" Matt. xvii. 25. "Is it lawful to give *tribute* unto Cæsar, or not?" Matt. xxii. 17. So when Jesus said (verse 19), "Shew me the *tribute*-money," they brought him a denarius; also Mark xii. 14.

Κοδράντης—Latin *quadrans*, from *quatuor*, four, i. e.,

the fourth part of an *as;* analogous to the English word with which it is translated, farthing, i. e., *fourthing.* "Thou shalt by no means come out thence till thou hast paid the uttermost *farthing*," Matt. v. 26. "And she threw in two mites (λεπτά), which make a *farthing.*" Mark xii. 42.

Κολωνία—Latin *colonia*, from *colere*, to cultivate, settle, occupy. The governments of the *coloniae* were modeled after that of the parent city Rome. Hence, in a *colonia*, Paul, as a Roman citizen, had a right to expect fair treatment. Regular Greek word κληρουχία. "Philippi, which is the chief city of that part of Macedonia, and a *colony.*" Acts xvi. 12.

Κουστωδία—Latin *custodia*, originally a watching, then a guard, from *custos*, a guard. Regular Greek word φυλακή. "Ye have a *watch* . . . sealing the stone and setting a *watch.*" Matt. xxvii. 65, 66. "Some of the *watch* came into the city." Matt. xxviii. 11.

Λεγεών—Latin *legio*, varying in number from three thousand three hundred to six thousand two hundred. Regular Greek word στρατόπεδον. "Shall presently give me more than twelve *legions* of angels?" Matt. xxvi. 53. "My name is Legion, for we are many." Mark v. 9, 15. Luke viii. 30. The word is used by Plutarch.

Λέντιον—Latin *linteum*, a linen cloth, from *linum*, linen, parallel with, or borrowed from, the Greek λίνον. Regular Greek word χειρόμακτρον. "He riseth from supper and laid aside his garments, and took a *towel* and girded himself." John xiii. 4, also verse 5.

Λίτρα—Evidence is given in Liddell and Scott's Lexicon that this is borrowed from the Latin *libra*. The substitution of τ for *b* seems strange, but we may compare the formative endings, Greek and Latin, -τρον, -*trum*, -*brum*, -*bra*. The regular Greek is μνᾶ. "Mary therefore took a *pound* of ointment," John xii. 3; "about a hundred *pound* weight," xix. 39.

Μάκελλον—Latin *macellum*, a meat-market,* plainly distinguished from *forum*, the Greek ἀγορά. The word supplied a real need in Greek. "Whatsoever is sold in the *shambles* eat." 1 Cor. x. 25.

Μεμβράνα—Latin *membrana*, a membrane, then parchment. Regular Greek διφθέρα, dressed hide. Περγαμηνή was also used, whence Latin *pergamena* and our *parchment*, the skin-paper originally from Pergamum. "And the books, but especially the *parchments*." 2 Tim. iv. 13.

Μίλιον—Latin *mille*, for *mille passuum*, a thousand paces. Polybius, Strabo and Plutarch use the word, and there seems to have been no equivalent native Greek word. "Whosoever shall compel thee to go one *mile*, go with him twain." Matt. v. 41.

Μόδιος—Latin *modius*, a peck-measure; unrepresented in pure Greek, except so far as ἕκτος, sixth, i. e., sixth part of a *medimmus*, represents it. "Neither do men light a lamp and put it under the *bushel*." Matt. v. 15. Parallel, Mark iv. 21; Luke xi. 33. The *modius*

---

*"Venio ad *macellum*, rogito pisces; indicant
Caros, agninam caram, caram bubulam,
Vitulinam, cetum, porcinam, cara omnia;
Atque eo fuerunt cariora; aes non erat."
   Plautus, Aulularia, Act ii., Scene 8, lines 3-6.

was like our bushel in being the unit of measure, but with only one-fourth of its capacity. The translation "bushel" was perhaps more needed with "candle" than with "lamp," when we consider the ancient form of the latter. Wyclif (Purvey) speaks of putting a "lanterne under a buschel."

Ξέστης, a corruption of the Latin *sextarius*, the *s* and *x* being interchanged, possibly under the influence of ξεστός, though ξ could represent ς, as in ξύν. "Washings of cups and *pots* and brazen vessels." Mark vii. 4. These pots were pint-measures. The Vulgate and Old Latin translated by *urceus*. Hill's Tatian has "measures."

Πραιτώριον—Latin *praetorium*, originally a general's tent, later, the prætorian guard, and a ruler's palace. From *praetor*. Nearest Greek word, αὐλή. "Then the soldiers of the governor took Jesus into the *palace*." Matt. xxvii. 27. "Within the court which is the Prætorium." Mark xv. 16. "Into the *palace*." John xviii. 28, 33; xix. 9. "Herod's *palace*." Acts xxiii. 35. "Throughout the whole *Prætorian guard*." Phil. i. 13.

Ῥέδη—Latin *rheda*, of Gallic origin, a four-wheeled carriage. The enumeration of the merchandise of Babylon includes "horses and *chariots*." Rev. xviii. 13. The *rheda* was not what we understand by the ancient chariot—*currus*, and ἅρμα—which was small, two-wheeled, and without seats, and used mostly in war. It was a roomy, comfortable carryall.

Σικάριος—Latin *sicarius*, from *sica*, a curved dagger. The

Romans considered the weapon unbecoming a gentleman. It was the badge of an assassin. Perhaps the nearest Greek word was σφαγεύς, butcher, cut-throat, but without the exact associations of *sicarius*. It was a Roman officer that said to Paul, "Art thou not then the Egyptian, which before these days stirred up to sedition and led out into the wilderness the four thousand men of the *Assassius?*" Acts xxi. 38.

Σιμικίνθιον—Latin *semicinctinm*. The etymology would seem to indicate a narrow skirt reaching half-way round, and thus properly rendered "apron," but there seems to be no other evidence that such a garment was worn. Martial has an epigram entitled "Semicinctium," in which the word is defined by *praecingere*,* where again etymology implies a fore-cloth, but the usage of the verb does not support the meaning. At Ephesus "unto the sick were carried away from [Paul's] body handkerchiefs or *aprons.*" Acts xix. 12.

Σουδάριον—Latin *sudarium*, sweat-cloth, from *sudor*, sweat. Regular Greek word καψιδρώτιον. The sudarium had as various use as our handkerchief, which means, literally, a head-cover carried in the hand. Napkin is early English for handkerchief. The Emperor Nero used to appear in public with a *sudarium* about his neck (Suetonius 51). "Lord, behold, here is thy pound, which I kept laid up in a *napkin.*" Luke xix. 20. "He that was dead [Lazarus] came forth, bound hand and foot with grave-clothes, and

---

* "Det tunicam dives; ego te praecingere possum.
  Essem si locuples, munus utrumque darem."—xiv. 153.

his face was bound about with a *napkin.*" John xi. 44.
"Beholdeth the linen cloths lying, and the *napkin* that was upon his head." John xx. 6, 7. "*Handkerchiefs* and aprons." Acts xix. 12.

Σπεκουλάτωρ—Latin *speculator*, from *speculari*, originally a scout; under the emperors, a member of the bodyguard, or adjutant. Regular Greek word σωματοφύλαξ. Herod, "the king, sent forth a *soldier of his guard*, and commanded to bring his head." Mark vi. 27.

Τίτλος—Latin *titulus*, an inscription. Regular Greek ἐπιγραφή, which is used both by Mark (xv. 26), and Luke (xxiii. 38). John gives a precise and graphic account of the inscription, mentioning its three languages, Pilate's authorship of it, and his curt refusal to change it. The evangelist may have caught his Latin word from the lips of the Roman governor himself. "Pilate wrote a *title* also, and put it on the cross. . . . This *title* therefore read many of the Jews." John xix. 19, 20. Suetonius—perhaps no earlier Latin author—uses *titulus* to denote the charge against a criminal. See two citations (Caligula 32, Domitian 10) in Thayer's Lexicon.

Φαινόλης (φαιλόνης, φελόνης)—Latin *paenula*, a woolen traveling cloak. The fashion of the garment was also borrowed, there being no exact Greek correspondence to word or thing. Χλαμύς is used by Matthew (xxvii. 28, 31) of the "scarlet *robe*" put in mockery on Jesus, while John (xix. 2) calls it ἱμάτιον, a word found much in the Gospels, and used in Plutarch for the Roman *toga*. Paul in his last epistle writes, "The *cloak*

that I left at Troas with Carpus bring when thou comest."
2 Tim. iv. 13. It was quite consistent with his need of
this warm over-garment that he should say (verse 21),
"Do thy diligence to come before winter."

Φραγέλλιον—Latin *flagellum*, diminutive from *flagrum*,
a whip. Regular Greek, μάστιξ, which is used Acts
xxii. 24 and Heb. xi. 36. "And he made a *scourge* of
cords." John ii. 15.

Φραγελλόω—Latin *flagello*. Regular Greek μαστιγόω,
which is generally used in the New Testament. "But
Jesus he *scourged* and delivered to be crucified." Matt.
xxvii. 26; parallel, Mark xv. 15.

Χῶρος—Latin *corus, caurus*, the northwest wind. Regular Greek ἀργέστης. The only occurrence of the
word is in the account of the harbor Phœnix, Acts xxvii.
12—λιμένα τῆς Κρήτης βλέποντα κατὰ λίβα καὶ κατὰ χῶρον.
The common version translates "and lieth toward
the south-west and *north-west.*" The revised version has "a haven of Crete looking north-east and *south-
east.*" This seems too much like trying to make the text
mean what it *ought* to, according to the topography of
the place; for the modern harbor opens towards the east.
The rendering is warmly advocated in Alford's commentary. The Revised margin has "Gr. down the south-
west wind, and down the north-west wind." Yet how
can we believe that looking κατὰ χῶρον means looking
with the *back to the wind?* See examples from the Septuagint in Thayer's Lexicon at the end of βλέπω. Ramsay
says: "It must be observed that Luke never saw the

harbor, and merely speaks on Paul's report of the professional opinion. It is possible that the sailors described the entrance as one in which the inward-bound ships looked towards N. W. and S.W., and that in transmission from mouth to mouth, the wrong impression was given that the harbor looked N. W. and S. W."* Coneybeare and Howson say: "The difficulty is to be explained simply by remembering that sailors speak of everything from their own point of view, and that such a harbor does 'look'—from the water towards the land which incloses it—in the direction of south-west and north-west."† Alford replies: "I cannot believe that even sailors could speak of a harbor as 'looking' in the direction in which *they* would look when entering it." But suppose we let the sailors go, and think only of what Luke, a landsman, might mean by his language. A small harbor is like a fort. A fort faces not its entrance, but in the direction in which its protecting guns point. So a harbor might be said to front the waves and winds which it keeps off. Its entrance might be in the rear or at one side, anywhere except at the front. It is true that a town, or a single house, on the inner shore of a harbor might face the entrance, and the open sea, but whether this is true of the harbor itself would depend on its shape; and in the absence of any settled usage, Luke might naturally refer to its sheltering power, with no thought of its entrance. He would then mean "sheltering from the S. W. and N. W. winds."

---

*"St. Paul the Traveler and the Roman Citizen," p. 326.
†"Life and Epistles of St. Paul," People's Ed., p. 741.

WORDS BORROWED FROM THE LATIN

To the foregoing Latin words should be added a half-Latin, εὐρακύλων (Acts xxvii. 14), from εὖρος and *Aquilo*, if that is the true reading instead of εὐροκλύδων; also λιβερτῖνος (Acts vi. 9), unless both are to be taken as proper names. Some examples of Latin influence in meaning and phraseology may be found in Thayer's Lexicon, Appendix, p. 693.

REMARKS.

1. The Latin words are twenty-six in number. The total number of words, exclusive of proper names, is about five thousand. When we think of the length of time during which the Greek-speaking world had been under the sway of Rome—from about a century and a half before Christ—we cannot but admire the power of literary resistance in the wonderfully self-sufficient Greek tongue, that Roman influence should force but one word in two hundred into this vocabulary. This impression is deepened by the small number of times each word is used. The following thirteen—κολωνία, μάκελλον, μεμβράνα, μίλιον, ξέστης, ῥέδη, σικάριος, σιμικίνθιον, σπεκουλάτωρ, τίτλος, φαινόλης, φραγέλλιον, χῶρος—are found but once. Of the rest, all but δηνάριον and πραιτώριον, are used from two to four times; but some of these are in parallel passages.

2. Classified grammatically, these words are all *nouns*, except one, φραγελλόω, which, indeed, is next door to a noun, being a denominative verb. This fact indicates that the reception of foreign words into the vocabulary

was in an early stage. Nouns come in first. The purity of even Xenophon's diction was not sullied by the free admission of such foreign substantives as παρασάγγης, δαρεικός, παράδεισος, and κάμηλος. A new thing from abroad requires a new name, and none can be better than its own. The history of our own language is to the point. Back in the Anglo-Saxon we find nouns (but few verbs) from Latin and Greek, as, *sacerde*, *pund* (pound), *mynster*, *mynet* (mint); by and by comes in the flood of verbs, adjectives, adverbs, as well as nouns, and now and then a preposition and conjunction, until the only grammatical territory we have left without invasion is the narrow one of pronouns. One can appreciate the condition of our New Testament vocabulary in this respect by looking on into later Greek, and finding such words as these—πραίσεντος (*praesens*), ἐκουῖνοςς (*equinus*), πραιπόσιτος (*praepositus*).

3. As to the meanings of these words, only one has reference to personal character, σικάριος; one to a vehicle, ῥέδη; one to a place of trade, μάκελλον; one to the wind, χῶρος; two to writing, μεμβράνα, τίτλος; four to measures, λίτρα, μίλιον, μόδιος, ξέστης; two to punishment, φραγέλλιον, φραγελλόω; three to coins, ἀσσάριον, δηνάριον, κοδράντης; three to civil life, κῆνσος, κολωνία, πραιτώριον; four to military life, κεντυρίων, κυυστωδία, λεγεών, σπεκουλάτωρ; four to articles of clothing and personal use, λέντιον, σιμικίνθιον, συυδάριον, φαινόλης. It will be seen from this that the remark of Winer, in his Grammar, that the Latin words in the New Testament are "mostly substantives

denoting Roman judicial institutions, coins, or articles of dress,"* needs considerable modification; not one of these words denotes a judicial institution, and those denoting coins and articles of dress are about a quarter of the whole number. Indeed, the absence of several Roman governmental terms is quite noticeable. Pontius Pilate, the procurator of Judæa, is ἡγεμών, not προκουράτωρ (Matt. xxvii. 2); the judgment-seat is βῆμα, not τριβουνάλιον (John xix. 13; Acts xxv. 6; Rom. xiv. 10, et al.); the colonial consul is στρατηγός, not κῶνσουλ (Acts xvi. 20); and his attendant lictor ῥαβδοῦχος—rod-holder—not λίκτωρ; Claudius Lysias, the military tribune—modern colonel —is χιλίαρχος, not τριβοῦνος. All of these Grecized Latin names are found in later Greek, and three of them in Plutarch, who lived but a half-century after the apostle John.

4. It may be well to distinguish the different *writers* of the New Testament in respect to the use of Latin words. Κουστωδία and μίλιον are used by Matthew only. Κεντυρίων, ξέστης, and σπεκουλάτωρ are used by Mark only. Instead of κεντυρίων, Matthew and Luke always use ἑκατοντάρχης, or ἑκατόνταρχος. Κολωνία, σικάριος, σιμικίνθιον, and χῶρος are used by Luke only. Λέντιον, λίτρα, ῥέδα, τίτλος, and φραγέλλιον are used by John only. Μάκελλον, μεμβράνα, and φαινόλης are used by Paul only. Κῆνσος, κοδράντης, and φραγελλόω are used by Matthew and Mark. Ἀσσάριον is used by Matthew and Luke. Σουδάριον is used by Luke and John. Λεγεών and μόδιος are used by

---
*P. 103 (Thayer's edition).

Matthew, Mark, and Luke. *Δηνάριον* is used by Matthew, Mark, Luke, and John. *Πραιτώριον* is used by Matthew, Mark, Luke, John, and Paul. No Latin words are found in Hebrews, Peter, James, and Jude. The words are so evenly distributed, if we except Paul, that our most important inference is that there is nothing to infer. As to number, Matthew uses ten, Mark ten, Luke ten, John eight, and Paul four. The most marked case of difference between the evangelists is in the word *κεντυρίων*, which is avoided by Matthew and Luke; by the latter both in his Gospel and the Acts. The subject-matter of Paul's Epistles would naturally make the use of Latin words less frequent.

5. Let us now, for the sake of a little comparison, take just a glance into the pages of a secular writer of the Roman period. Polybius, born about 200. B. C., was both the first and foremost Greek writer of this period. Notwithstanding his experience of the iron hand of Rome, he became, under the fostering friendship of the younger Scipio, an ardent admirer of Roman institutions, and made it the great task of his life to compose the history of Rome. His subject would be likely to bring in all the Latin words which a legitimate vocabulary would allow; yet the consul is called *ὕπατος* (or *στρατηγός*, as in the New Testament; in which, also, we find *ἀνθύπατος*, for proconsul (Acts xiii. 7, et al.)); the lictor, *ῥαβδοῦχος*; the military tribune, *χιλίαρχος*; the tribune of the plebs, *δήμαρχος*; the censor, *τιμητής*; the quæstor, *ταμίας*; the legion, *στρατόπεδον*; the senate, *σύγκλητος* or *συνέδριον*,

not σενᾶτος, as in Plutarch. Two of the New Testament Latin words,—μίλιον and κεντυρίων,—and perhaps others of them, are in Polybius; but with κεντυρίων is found also ταξίαρχος; and other designations of officers are duplicated, as δεκάδαρχος and δεκουρίων, ὕπαρχος and πραίφεκτος. Indeed, in the case of one word, which must have been very suggestive to Polybius and his Greek compatriots,—Δικτάτωρ,—we can almost trace its progress into the vocabulary. In the narrative of the Second Punic War, the author states that the Romans had come to need a general with unlimited powers—αὐτοκράτωρ στρατηγός. In the next chapter he states that they appointed Quintus Fabius Δικτάτωρ, and goes on to explain the powers of this extraordinary officer. The Greek of Polybius, like that of the New Testament, was slow to admit the vocabulary of the Romans.

6. This discussion points to the *genuineness* of the Greek of the New Testament. Latin words so few, so unimportant, and so seldom used—and that too in circumstances where they would be likely to be used—indicate that the writers of the New Testament could "speak Greek." But there is another conclusion, of a more special character. The Latin element of the New Testament vocabulary indicates the *early composition* of the books of the New Testament. The Roman period of Greek literature extends from 146 B. C. to 330 A. D.; but for the New Testament it would be more fair to substitute 60 B. C. for the former date. Our Latin test, then, would place these books early in the period thus

limited. Their Latin is more like that of Polybius than it is like that of Plutarch even. Plutarch uses κώνσουλ, λίκτωρ, τριβοῦνος, σενᾶτος, ἤδικτον, πατρίκιος, λίτυον; besides six of the New Testament words—ἀσσάριον, δηνάριον, λεγεών, λίτρα, μάκελλον, μίλιον.

PROPER NAMES.

The following is a list of proper names, with single references. A few, as 'Ρώμη, first appear in literature in a Greek dress, but must have come from Roman lips.

'Αγρίππας, *Agrippa*, Acts xxv. 13; 'Αμπλίας, *Ampliatus*, enlarged, Rom. xvi. 8; 'Ακύλας, *Aquila*, eagle, Acts xviii. 2; 'Αππίου Φόρον, *Appii Forum*, Forum of Appius, Acts xxviii. 15; 'Απφία, *Appia*, Phil. 2; Αὔγουστος, *Augustus*, reverend, Luke ii. 1; Γαλλίων, *Gallio*, Gallic, Acts xviii. 12; Δρούσιλλα, *Drusilla*, diminutive of Drusus, Acts xxiv. 24; Εὐρακύλων, *Euro-aquilo*, northeast wind, Acts xxvii. 14; 'Ιουλία, *Julia*, feminine of Julius, Rom. xvi. 15; 'Ιούλιος, *Julius*, Acts xxvii. 1; 'Ιουνίας, *Junia*, youthful, Rom. xvi. 7; 'Ιοῦστος, *Justus*, just, Acts i. 23; 'Ιταλία, *Italia*, Acts xviii. 2; Καῖσαρ, *Cæsar*, long-haired, Matt. xxii. 17; Καισάρεια, *Cæsarea*, Cæsar's city, Matt. xvi. 13; Κλαυδία, *Claudia*, limping, 2 Tim. iv. 21; Κλαύδιος, *Claudius*, limping, Acts xi. 28; Κλήμης, *Clemens*, kind, Phil. iv. 3; Κορνήλιος, *Cornelius*, Acts x. 1; Κούαρτος, *Quartus*, fourth, Rom. xvi. 23; Κρήσκης, *Crescens*, growing, 2 Tim. iv. 10; Κρίσπος, *Crispus*, curly-haired, Acts xviii. 8; Λιβερτῖνοι, *Libertini*, freedmen, Acts vi. 9; Λούκιος, *Lucius*, day-light man (*lux*), Acts xiii. 1; Μάρκος, *Marcus*, hammer, Acts xii. 12; Νίγερ, *Niger*, black, Acts xiii. 1; Οὐρβανός, *Urbanus*, city-man, Rom. xvi. 9; Παῦλος, *Paulus*, little, Acts xiii. 7, 9; Πιλᾶτος, *Pilatus*, javelin-man (*pilum*), Matt. xxvii. 2; Πόντιος, *Pontius*, bridge-man, Matt. xxvii. 2; Πόπλιος, *Publius*, the people's, Acts xxviii. 7; Πόρκιος, *Porcius*, swine-man? Acts xxiv. 27; Ποτίολοι, *Puteoli*, little wells, Acts xxviii. 13; Πούδης, *Pudens*, modest, 2 Tim. iv. 21; Πρίσκα, *Prisca*, old, 2 Tim. iv. 19; Πρίσκιλλα, *Priscilla*, diminutive of Prisca, Acts xviii. 2; Ῥοῦφος, *Rufus*, red-haired, Mark xv. 21; Ῥώμη, *Roma*, Acts xviii. 2; Σεκοῦνδος, *Secundus*, second, Acts xx. 4; Σέργιος, *Sergius*, Acts xiii. 7; Σίλας, *Silas*, shortened from the following, Acts xv. 22; Σιλουανός, *Silvanus*, woodsman, 2 Cor. i. 19; Σπανία, *Hispania*, Rom. xv. 24; Τέρτιος, *Tertius*, third, Rom. xvi. 23; Τέρτυλλος, *Tertullus*, Acts xxiv. 1; Τιβεριάς, *Tiberias*, city of Tiberias, John vi. 1; Τιβέριος, *Tiberius*, Tiber-man, Luke iii. 1; Τίτος, *Titus*, 2 Cor. ii. 13; Τρεῖς Ταβέρναι, *Tres Tabernae*, three shops, Acts xxviii. 15; Φῆλιξ, *Felix*, happy, Acts xxiii. 24; Φῆστος, *Festus*, feast-day, Acts xxiv. 27; Φορτουνᾶτος, *Fortunatus*, fortunate, 1 Cor. xvi. 17.

Of this array of names the Christian mind dwells longest on one which, as we have it in English, hardly suggests a Roman origin, but is really a famous name in Roman history—Παῦλος. From the time of the Christian Fathers to the present, conjecture has done its best to answer the question, Why did Saul assume the name Paulus? and this in spite of the fact that it is nowhere affirmed that he *did* assume it, instead of receiving it from his father when he was "free-born." The Greek text gives us the least possible information on this point. Σαῦλος δέ, ὁ καὶ Παῦλος (Acts xiii. 9) is all. If he did not get the name from his father, some have thought that he did from the proconsul of Cyprus, Sergius Paulus; others from his being *little* of stature; others from his humility, he being, in his own estimation, "the *least* of all saints." If his father named him Παῦλος, we can imagine two or three good reasons. 1. It was an honored name. L. Æmilius Paulus honored it at Cannæ, to whom Horace applies the phrase *animae magnae prodigus;* and the conqueror of Macedonia, the father of the younger Scipio, sustained well the honor of his ancestor. 2. It was a name well known in the East. The Paulus last mentioned bore as his agnomen "Macedonicus," and did more than any other one to make Greece a part of the Roman world. 3. It resembled Saul more than any other Roman surname; and yet we cannot tell which name of the two was first decided upon. But whether any of these reasons are valid or not, the appearance of this name at the beginning of Paul's apostolic life justifies us in regarding it as his distinctively Christian and missionary name. Ramsay, under the heading "Saul, otherwise Paul," while courteously deriding Weizsäcker for regarding the two names as a sign of double authorship of the Acts, remarks, " Amid the conflict of the two religions before the Roman governor, Paul stepped forward in his character of citizen of the Empire." (St. Paul, etc., p.

85.) He illustrates Paul's names by the custom among certain non-Greek races of having two names, one native and the other Greek. "The *role* he was playing for the time being determined which name he was called by."

One might expect many Latin names in the greetings of an epistle to the church at Rome; but of the twenty-six who are greeted in the last chapter of Romans, only seven—Prisca, Aquila, Junias, Amplias (-atus), Urbane (Urbanus), Rufus, and Julia—bear Roman names; while four such join in the greeting—Lucius, Tertius, Caius (Gaius), and Quartus.

XVII

WORDS BORROWED FROM THE HEBREW AND ARAMAIC

Τὸ λεγόμενον Ἑβραϊστί. John v. 2.

THE great number of Old Testament proper names thrust upon New Testament Greek—a large proportion without inflection—give a Hebrew coloring to the text far beyond what comes from the legitimate vocabulary. The first chapter of Matthew, and the third of Luke, and, elsewhere, such unconformable words as Ἀβραάμ Ἰσαάκ, Ἰακώβ make one feel that grammatically the Old Testament is going rough-shod over the New. But these names do not correctly represent the case. In studying the borrowed vocabulary we may set aside proper names, and two other classes; (1) those words which are quoted as from a foreign language, and translated, (2) those Semitic words which are found also in the classical period. It may be well, however, to mention the words of these two classes, though they are ruled out.

Those of the first class are the following:

Ἐλωί—Aramaic אֱלָהִי, for the Hebrew אֵלִי, from אֵל, *God*, with the suffix י—, *my*, "My God." Mark xv. 34.

Ἐφφαθά—Aram. אֶתְפְּתַח, imperative middle from פְּתַח, *to open;* "Be opened." Mark vii. 34.

Ἠλί—See Ἐλωί above. "My God." Matt. xxvii. 46.

Κοῦμι—Hebrew, קוּמִי, imperative feminine, from קוּם, to *rise.* "Arise." Mark v. 41.

Λεμά, Λαμᾶ—Heb. לָמָה, from the preposition לְ, *for*, and מָה, *what*. "Why?"

Σαβαχθανί—Chaldee, שְׁבַקְתַּנִי, second person singular from שְׁבַק, *to leave*, with the verbal personal suffix נִי-, *me*. With Λαμᾶ, above, "Why hast thou forsaken me?" Matt. xxvii. 46; Mark xv. 34.

Ταλιθά—Aram. טַלִיתָא, "damsel." Mark v. 41.

The words of Semitic origin which are found also in the classics are the following (the Hebrew word being annexed as the best accessible representative of the Semitic original):

Ἀῤῥαβών—עֵרָבוֹן, *earnest-money*, from עָרַב, *to pledge*. Hence the Latin *arhabo*, *arrha*, and *rhabo*, found as early as Plautus. This word is found three times in the New Testament, used by Paul; "*Earnest* of the Spirit." 2 Cor. i. 22; v. 5. "*Earnest* of our inheritance." Eph. i. 14.

Βύσσος—בּוּץ, from a root meaning *white*. "Was clothed in purple and *fine linen*." Luke xvi. 19. "Merchandise . . . . . of pearls and *fine linen*." Rev. xviii. 12.

Κάμηλος—גָּמָל, *a camel*. Used of the raiment of John the Baptist (Matt. iii. 4; Mark i. 6), and in the sayings about going through the eye of a needle (Matt. xix. 24; Mark x. 25; Luke xviii. 25), and swallowing a camel. Matt. xxiii. 24.

Κιννάμωμον—קִנָּמוֹן, *cinnamon*. "No man buyeth . . . . *cinnamon* and odors." Rev. xviii. 13.

Κύμινον—כַּמֹּן, *cummin*. "Tithe of mint, anise, and *cummin*." Matt. xxiii. 23.

Λίβανος—לְבֹנָה, *frankincense*, from לָבֵן, *to be white*.

"*Frankincense* and myrrh." Matt. ii. 11. "No man buyeth... *frankincense* and wine." Rev. xviii. 13.

Λιβανωτός—derived from the preceding, is found in Herodotus in the same sense, but is used in the New Testament in a different sense. "Holding a golden *censer*." Rev. viii. 3, 5.

Σάπφειρος—סַפִּיר, *sapphire*, from סָפַר, *to scrape*. "The second [foundation was] *sapphire*." Rev. xxi. 19.

Συκάμινος—שִׁקְמָה, *a sycamore tree*. "Ye might say unto this *sycamine tree*." Luke xvii. 6.

Ὕσσωπος—אֵזוֹב, *hyssop*. "Put it upon *hyssop*." John xix. 29. "Scarlet wool and *hyssop*." Heb. ix. 19.

To these ten should perhaps be added ἄλφα, אָלֶף (Rev. i. 8, 11; xxi. 6; xxii. 13), and ἰῶτα, יוֹד, "jot" (Matt. v. 18).

Dismissing now the words thus enumerated, we come to those which are introduced by the writers without an avowed translation, and which are not found in classical Greek. The translations are from the common version.

'Αββᾶ—Aramaic אַבָּא, corresponding to the Hebrew אָב, *father*. "And he said, *Abba*, Father, all things are possible unto thee; take away this cup from me." Mark xiv. 36. "Ye have received the spirit of adoption, whereby we cry, *Abba*, Father." Rom. viii. 15. "God hath sent forth the spirit of his son into your hearts, crying, *Abba*, Father." Gal. iv. 6. It will be seen that "ἀββᾶ, πατήρ" are always joined together, and one might say at first glance that the latter is simply a translation; but this is quite inconsistent with the spirit of the second and third passages. Paul would hardly recommend a lesson in translation as a cry of filial love. "Abba, Father" means more than "Father," and why, if not from association with those words in Gethsemane, some of whose very syllables passed from heart to heart, and were preserved for us by the faithful and exact Mark? A Greek-speaking Jew, if he chose to retain ἀββᾶ, would naturally add πατήρ, especially if in the anguish of the hour the ἀββᾶ were twice repeated. It would appear, then, that in the account of Mark πατήρ is virtually a translation, but that the two words, once joined, represented ever after the tenderest and deepest filial spirit. Luther's "Lieber Vater" was not far from right.

Ἀλληλούϊα—Hebrew הַלְלוּ־יָהּ, from הַלְלוּ, *praise ye*, and יָהּ, a shortened form of Jehovah or Yahveh—*Praise ye Jehovah*. This word occurs four times, and in the book where we look for the fervor of ancient prophecy and psalm. "I heard a great voice of much people in heaven, saying, *Alleluia*." Rev. xix. 1; also in verses 3, 4 and 6.

Ἀμήν—Hebrew אָמֵן, *firm*, from אָמֵן, *to support*. Used often by our Savior, as reported by all the evangelists, as an adverb of affirmation, "verily," duplicated by John only, "Verily, verily,"—once by Paul in a similar sense, "For all the promises of God in him are yea, and in him *Amen*." 2 Cor. i. 20. Used, according to the textus receptus, many times as an exclamatory prayer, "Amen"; but in a majority of cases the reading is disputed.

Βάτος—(masculine), Heb. בַּת, *a bath*, a liquid measure of about eight and one-half gallons. Used only once. "How much owest thou unto my lord? And he said, A hundred *measures* of oil." Luke xvi. 5, 6.

Γέεννα—Heb. גֵי־הִנֹּם, *valley of Hinnom*, from גַּיְא, *valley*, and הִנֹּם, *Hinnom*, a valley on the south and west of Jerusalem in which was Topheth (2 Kings xxiii. 10). This word is found in Matthew, Mark, Luke and James, as follows: "In danger of *hell*-fire." Matt. v. 22. "Whole body should be cast into *hell*." v. 29, also verse 30. "Destroy both soul and body in *hell*." x. 28. "Having two eyes to be cast into *hell-fire*." xviii. 9; also Mark ix. 47. "Two-fold more the child of *hell* than yourselves." xxiii. 15. "How can ye escape the damnation of *hell?*" xxiii. 33. "Than having two hands to go into *hell*." Mark ix. 43. "Than having two feet to be cast into *hell*." ix. 45. "Fear him which after he hath killed hath power to cast into *hell*." Luke xii. 5. "It is set on fire of *hell*." James iii. 6.

Ἑβραϊστί—from ἑβραΐζω, *to speak Hebrew*, from עֵבֶר, *Eber, Heber;* a word used by John only. "*Called in the Hebrew tongue*, Bethesda." John v. 2; also xix. 13, 17, 20; Rev. ix. 11; xvi. 16. The words Ἑβραϊκός, Ἑβραῖος, and Ἑβραΐς may be classed as proper names.

Ἰουδαΐζω—from יְהוּדָה, Judah. Used only once. "Why compellest thou the Gentiles *to live as do the Jews?*" Gal. ii. 14.

Ἰουδαϊκῶς—from the same through Ἰουδαϊκός. Used only once. "Livest after the manner of the Gentiles and not *as do the Jews*." Gal. ii. 14.

Ἰουδαϊσμός—from Ἰουδαΐζω. Used twice. "My conversation in time past in the *Jews' religion*." Gal. i. 13. "And profited in the *Jews' religion*." i. 14. Ἰουδαϊκός and Ἰουδαῖος may be classed as proper names.

Κορβᾶν, κορβανᾶς—Heb. קָרְבָּן, *an offering;* used over seventy times in Leviticus and Numbers, in our version "offering" or "oblation," Septuagint, δῶρον. The indeclinable form κορβᾶν is translated by Mark, but Matthew uses κορβανᾶς without explanation. Each is used only once. "It is not lawful for to put them into the *treasury*." Matt. xxvii. 6. "But ye say, If a man shall say to his father or mother, It is *Corban*, that is to say, a gift." Mark vii. 11.

Κόρος—Heb. כֹּר, *a cor* (translated "measure" in our version, 1 Kings v. 11), a measure equal to ten baths. See βάτος, above. Used only once. "And how much owest thou? And he said, A hundred measures of wheat." Luke xvi. 7.

Μαμωνᾶς—Chaldee, מָמוֹנָא. Alford quotes from Augustine,"Lucrum Punice mammon dicitur." Used four times. "Ye cannot serve God and *mammon*." Matt. vi. 24. "Make to yourselves friends of the *mammon* of unrighteousness." "If, therefore, ye have not been faithful in the unrighteous *mammon*." "Ye cannot serve God and *mammon*." Luke xvi. 9, 11, 13.

Μάννα—Heb. מָן, a resinous manna, to which the miraculous manna undoubtedly bore some resemblance (Ex. xvi. 15). Used four times. "Our fathers did eat *manna* in the desert." John vi. 31; also 49. "Wherein was the golden pot that had *manna*." Heb. ix. 4. "To him that overcometh will I give to eat of the hidden *manna*." Rev. ii. 17.

Μαρὰν ἀθά—Aram. אָתָה, *to come*, and מָרָן, or מָרְנָא, *Lord*. The Lord comes. Used only once. "If any man love not the Lord Jesus Christ, let him be Anathema *Maran-atha*." 1 Cor. xvi. 22.

Πάσχα, Heb. פֶּסַח, *the passover*, from פָּסַח, *to pass over*. This word is used in each of the four Gospels, referring to the literal festival, it being always translated in our version "Passover"; also once in Acts xii. 4, where it is mistranslated (to modern ears) "Easter." It is found also in the two following: "For even Christ our *Passover* is sacrificed for us." 1 Cor. v. 7. "Through faith he kept the *Passover*." Heb. xi. 28.

Προσάββατον, from *σάββατον*. See below. Used once only. "Because it was the preparation, that is, the *day before the Sabbath*." Mark xv. 42.

'Ραββί, Heb. רַבִּי, from רַב, *great man, master*, and suffix ִי—, *my*. Used frequently in the Gospels, not in Luke. "And to be called of men *Rabbi, Rabbi*." Matt. xxiii. 7. "Then Judas which betrayed him answered and said, *Master*, is it I?" Matt. xxvi. 25. Nine times it is in our version "Master"; at other times "Rabbi." It is translated " *Διδάσκαλε*" once by John (i. 39).

'Ραββουνί—perhaps not differing in meaning from Rabbi. Used twice, being translated by John, but used by Mark without explanation. "The blind man said unto him, *Lord*, that I might receive my sight." Mark

x. 51. "She turned herself and saith unto him, Rabboni, which is to say, *Master.*" John xx. 16.

'Ραxά—Aram. רֵיקָא, corresponding to the Heb. רֵיק, *empty.* Used only once. "Whosoever shall say to his brother, *Raca*, shall be in danger of the council." Matt. v. 22.

Σαβαώθ—Heb. צְבָאוֹת, *of hosts*, the genitive plural being transferred to the Greek. Used twice, the first being a translation from the Septuagint of Isa. i. 9. "Except the Lord of *Sabaoth* had left us a seed." Rom. ix. 29. "The cries of them which have reaped have entered into the ears of the Lord of *Sabaoth*." James v. 4.

Σαββατισμός, from σαββατίζω, from σάββατον. See the following. Used only once. "There remaineth therefore a *rest* to the people of God." Heb. iv. 9.

Σάββατον—Heb. שַׁבָּת, a *Sabbath*, from שָׁבַת, *to rest.* Used often in the Gospels and Acts, and in the following: "Upon the first day of the *week* let every one of you lay by him in store." 1 Cor. xvi. 2. "Of the new moon or of the *Sabbath.*" Col. ii. 16.

Σάτον—Aram. סָאתָא, Heb. סְאָה, *a seah*, a dry measure of about a peck and a half; in our version simply "measure." Gen. xviii. 6. Used twice. "Leaven which a woman took and hid in three *measures* of meal." Matt. xiii. 33. See Luke xiii. 21.

Σίκερα—Heb. שֵׁכָר, *intoxicating drink*, from שָׁכַר, *to be drunken.* ("Do not drink wine nor *strong drink*." Lev. x. 9.) Used only once. "Shall drink neither wine nor *strong drink.*" Luke i. 15.

Χερουβίμ, Χερουβείν—Heb. כְּרוּב, *cherub*, plural כְּרוּבִים, *cherubim*. Used only once. "And over it the *cherubim* of glory." Heb. ix. 5.

Ὡσαννά—from Heb. הוֹשִׁיעָה נָא, *save now*, from יָשַׁע, *to be safe*, and נָא, *now*, a particle of exhortation. ("*Save now*, I beseech thee, O Lord." Ps. cxviii. 25.) Used three times by Matthew, twice by Mark, and once by John, all concerning one occasion. "The multitudes that went before, and that followed, cried, saying, Hosanna to the Son of David." Matt. xxi. 9. Not used by Luke or other New Testament writers.

To these should perhaps be added ζιζάνιον (Matt. xiii., seven times in the parable of the tares).

REMARKS.

1. The Hebraistic character of New Testament Greek does not come largely from its Hebrew *words*. The word which makes the strongest impression upon the cursory reader is Ἀμήν, especially as solemnly reiterated in John's Gospel. But this in the Gospels is given as the utterance of one who spoke in a language foreign to Greek. It is also exclamatory, and on its face bears evidence of being but imperfectly incorporated into the vocabulary. The same may be said of ἀββᾶ, Ἀλληλούϊα, κορβᾶν, μαρὰν ἀθά, ῥαββί, ῥαββουνί, ῥακά, σαβαώθ, χερουβίμ, and Ὡσαννά. Several are found only once, βάτος, Ἰουδαΐζω, Ἰουδαϊκῶς, κόρος, μαρὰν ἀθά, προσάββατον, ῥακά, σαββατισμός, σίκερα, and χερουβίμ.

The only words which occur with any frequency, and

which have in all respects the treatment of native words, are γέεννα, and σάββατον; but the former is used but once out of the first three Gospels. These borrowed words, then, go but a little way in revealing the presence of Hebrew influence. Yet they are a convenient starting-point for investigation, and their existence makes certain a multitude of Hebraisms, of a less obtrusive character, consisting of changes of meaning in single words, and the adoption of Hebrew constructions and phraseology.

2. How many of these words are found in the Septuagint, including the Apocrypha? There are sixteen, viz., Ἀλληλούϊα, ἀμήν, βάτος, Ἰουδαΐζω, Ἰουδαϊκῶς, Ἰουδαϊσμός, κόρος, μάννα, πάσχα, προσάββατον, σαβαώθ, σάββατον, σάτον, σίκερα, χερουβίμ, and the proper name Γαιέννα, used in Josh. xviii. 16, as a strictly geographical designation, for which elsewhere is found φάραγξ Ἐννόμ (Josh. xv. 8) and γὲ Βενεννόμ (2 Chron. xxviii. 3). The originals of these are pure Hebrew. Of the remainder the following are from the Aramaic: ἀββᾶ, μαρὰν ἀθά, ῥακά, σάτον, and probably Ὡσαννά, for the Jewish multitude in employing this word seem nòt so much to be quoting from the Psalms as using a familiar interjection.

That no more of these words are found in the Septuagint is what we ought to expect; for the language of the New Testament is not a book-dialect made up by students of the Septuagint, but the genuine speech of the people, growing by adopting new forms, as ἀββᾶ, or taking a word of narrow meaning and expanding it to reach beyond this world, like γέεννα.

3. It should be noticed that but few of these words touch important doctrine. Six are titles of respect or expressions of emotion, ἀββᾶ, Ἀλληλούϊα, ἀμήν, ῥαββί, ῥαββουνί, ῥακά, and Ὡσαννά. Three are measures, Βάτος, κόρος, and σάτον. Seven are purely historical, Ἑβραϊστί, Ἰουδαΐζω, Ἰουδαϊκῶς, Ἰουδαϊσμός, προσάββατον, σίκερα and χερουβίμ. Five are used in the enforcement of duty, κορβάν, μαμωνᾶς, μάννα, μαρὰν ἀθά, σαβαώθ. Ἀββᾶ, πάσχα, σαββατισμός, and σάββατον have doctrinal reference, but not prominently; thus leaving γέεννα as the one doctrinal word, standing out in awful distinctness as the word of doom.

4. A word in regard to the presence of Hebrew and Aramaic words in other late Greek writers. Josephus uses βάτος, Ἰουδαΐζω, Ἰουδαϊκῶς, κορβᾶν, κόρος, μάννα, πάσχα, σάββατον, σάτον, and χερουβίμ, besides others not found in the New Testament. The words which have gained currency by association with the life of Jesus we should not expect to find in Josephus. The Greek Christian Fathers took up and bore on most of them in a course that has reached our day, ἀββᾶ, Ἀλληλούϊα, ἀμήν, γέεννα, κορβᾶν, μαμωνᾶς, μάννα, πάσχα, σάββατον, χερουβίμ and Ὡσαννά.

5. Almost all of the personal names are, of course, found in the Old Testament, the most notable exception being Ἐλισάβετ (Elizabeth). Two precious names, Ἰησοῦς, Μαρία, do not at first glance show their Hebrew origin. Joshua, or Jehoshua, in its later form is Jeshua, or Yeshua. Remembering that *sh* must be represented in Greek by σ, and long u by ου, we have Ἰησουα, which by partial inflection becomes Ἰησοῦς. The name Μαρία,

Maria, is curiously set off by an unphilological imagination in the Latin Hymns as derived from *mare*, the sea, — " Ave maris stella." But we must rather identify it, as its other form Μαρίαμ shows, with the Miriam of the Red Sea song, even if her name does mean "rebellion." The Miriam is lost in the Mary.

XVIII

WORDS NOT FOUND IN CLASSICAL WRITERS

THAT the New Testament, as late Greek, should contain many unborrowed words not used in the classics is a matter of course. A valuable discussion of many of them and of the period is found in Kennedy's "Sources of New Testament Greek." There is a complete list in the Appendix to Thayer's Lexicon, Sections I. and II., Aristotle being included among classical writers. A nearly complete list is in the Bibliotheca Sacra for July and October, 1880, containing also the number of times used, and the words in the common version to translate each.

The following are some points of interest:

1. The number of these words is large, about nine hundred in all, exclusive of proper names—amounting to one-sixth of the whole vocabulary. The interval of time between the classics and the New Testament is not much greater than between the Elizabethan literature and our own. What would a literary critic say of a book, or a series of connected booklets, of to-day, every sixth word of which—repetitions not being counted—could not be found in Bacon or Hooker, or Spenser, or Shakespeare, or the contemporary English Bible, or in any earlier writing?—this book not to be special or technical, but designed for general popular use, and the new words to

be not borrowed from any foreign tongue during the last three hundred years. Our literary condition in this respect we account for by the printing-press, by the permanent interest of subject-matter, by creative genius, by the unity of our history, and by the reading-habit and linguistic study of modern civilization. Aside from the absence of modern conditions, both the newness and the nativeness of New Testament Greek can be explained by (1) the genius of the Greek language, growing by self-multiplication, (2) the break of continuity in Greek life, (3) the wide extension of Greek thought under Roman rule, and (4) the influence of Jewish thought centering in the Septuagint version of the Old Testament.

2. In regard to the etymological character of these words, they are, with very few exceptions, derivatives or compounds, and from roots found in the Greek classics. Nor are many of them at all obscure in origin. The relation of the noun ἀγάπη to the verb ἀγαπάω may be thought doubtful, but the connection of the two is not. The verb is used from Homer down to New Testament times. The first appearance of the noun in literature is in the Septuagint. How came it there? Deissmann has shown* that the word was in some use in Egypt independently of the Septuagint. As a rule, verbs in -άω imply nouns in -η in actual use, but it is extremely improbable that ἀγάπη could have been in general use so long without once appearing in the remains of the classics. It seems to have been latent in the verb. In general, among nouns the

---

*Bibelstudien, p. 80, Marburg, 1895.

large proportion of the heavier suffixes, as -μος (29), -μα (44), -σις (51), will be noticed, just as in English -*ness* and -*ship* have now a vigorous life at the expense of the lighter abstract endings; for word-making is a more conscious and obtrusive process as language grows older. The verbs are largely denominatives, but more largely multiplied by composition with prepositions, all of which are represented, except ἀμφί and εἰς. The adjectives arise mostly from composition, the frequency of ἀν- *privative* being noticeable, just as the English compounds with *un-* are constantly increasing. Without discussing this subject, we may safely assert that etymologically these words, as a class, are above reproach. The zeal of a Phrynichus may pronounce some of them "shockingly un-Attic"—δεινῶς ἀνάττικον—(and is not the charge true of his own expression?) but we must remember that those ancient-modern grammarians decided according to usage, not science. Words which to their ears were as painful as our present vocabulary would have been to Chaucer, may yet be accepted by us as belonging to the regular development of the language. The adverb πάντοτε, for example, was an offense to them, but seems so suitable and regular that we can hardly believe that we never saw it in classic authors. The reforming grammarians were determined to have the language both alive and dead at the same time. It has been said by later authorities that many of the compound verbs in the New Testament are nowise different in meaning from the simple verbs. But we should be slow to make a charge against New Testament Greek which could be perhaps equally well sustained against the Latin of such a master of style as Cicero. A mere increase of volume in a word may be made expressive. Then, too, the very nicest distinctions are next door to no distinction at all.

3. The rhetorical value of these words varies much. Some of the compound words have been thoroughly endorsed by modern usage, as ὀφθαλμοδουλεία, δίψυχος, and the compounds with ἀγαθο-, ἀντι-, ἑτερο-, and ψευδο-. Καρδιογνώστης, λογομαχία, μακροθυμία, and θεοδίδακτος, are certainly clear and full of meaning, and the list of like words could be greatly extended. What Greek word has rhetorically a better right to exist than σύνψυχος? Is it not finer than the corresponding Latin *con-cor-s*, which may possibly have given rise to it? (Did Paul coin the word? and did he learn Latin at Rome, where the epistle containing this word was written?) But few, we think, can be condemned, as perhaps μοσχοποιέω, and some other verbs in -έω, while of course a large majority are neither above nor below the ordinary level of expression.

4. How about the doctrinal and practical importance of the words? It is not to be expected that the founders of a new religion would endanger the communication of their truths by the needless employment of new words. The old words must first bear all the strain that they are capable of. The idea of God required no new word, and even the two words for Godhead, θειότης and θεότης, are each found but once. The word θέλημα for βουλή,

seems rather a matter of habit than necessity. Yet it is not without significance that we find such words as ἀποκάλυψις, ἀπολύτρωσις, ἁμαρτωλός, ἱλασμός, ἱλαστήριος, παλινγενεσία, ἀφθαρσία, and the five from ἀγαθός, as well as βάπτισμα, βαπτισμός, βαπτιστής, and other words of almost technical import. Perhaps the most remarkable of all are two which stand at the opposite poles of Christianity—the words for *love* and *conscience*. For love we find, never ἔρως, but always ἀγάπη; not *amor*, but *caritas*. That συνείδησις is not found in earlier Greek is not due to the absence of the idea of conscience, for that idea is expressed by verbal forms of σύνοιδα, but may possibly come from reluctance to form a verbal noun from an irregular preteritive verb, or, more probably, from less call for the use of such a word. One must be careful not to infer too much from the appearance of a new word. E. g. δεισιδαιμονία is late Greek, but its immediate parent δεισιδαίμων is in Xenophon's Cyropaedia; and μαθητεύω is late, but μαθητής is common in classical times. In many cases the most that can be inferred is that the word is the result of greater prominence of the idea, or more frequent use; but very often this would be saying too much, there being nothing to it but etymological convenience. Each case must be determined on its own merits.

5. The large number of these words found in the Septuagint is a matter of course—three hundred and sixty-three in all, of which, however, eight are used only in express citations, viz., αἰχμαλωτεύω, ἀνάβλεψις, ἐλαττονέω, ἐνευλογέομαι, κατάνυξις, καταφρονητής, παραπικρασμός, φρυάσσω.

The proportion, *two-fifths*, will not seem large when we consider the relation of Christianity to Judaism. The New Testament diction is not a servile copy of that of the Septuagint. Even such words as εἰδωλολατρεία, and μαθητεύω, are not found in the latter. A large proportion of the most striking compound words of the New Testament are also absent. Συνείδησις occurs but once in the Canonical Old Testament (Eccl. x. 20), and then with a different meaning ("Curse not the king, no, not in thy *thought* [מַדָּע]"). What the proportion might have been if the Septuagint had not been restricted by being a translation we cannot know. That this translation is of great value in interpreting the New Testament will not be denied by any one.

6. It would be interesting to compare the different authors and books of the New Testament, in respect to their use of late words. Let us glance at one book, the one that stands first in order among the Epistles in Tischendorf's edition, and which, according to some scholars, is the oldest of New Testament writings—the Epistle of James. As this is the only book that can with confidence be dated at Jerusalem, and as the author, whichever James he was, probably never went beyond the boundaries of Palestine, we should expect the widest divergence from classic Greek. Going through the Epistle in order, we meet with late words as follows: Chap. i. διασπορά (vs. 1), πειρασμός (2), ἀνεμίζω (6), δίψυχος (8), καύσων (11), πειρασμός (12), ἀπείραστος (13), ἀποκυέω (15), ἀποσκίασμα (17), ἀποκυέω (18), κτίσμα (18), περισσεία

(21), πραΰτης (21), ἐπιλησμονή (25), θρῆσκος (26), χαλιναγωγέω (26), θλίψις (27), ἄσπιλος (27). Chap. ii. προσωποληψία (1), χρυσοδακτύλιος (2), ὑποπόδιον (3), προσωπολημπτέω (9), ἀνέλεος (13), θυσιαστήριον (21). Chap. iii. χαλιναγωγέω (2), σπιλόω (6), πραΰτης (13), κατακαυχάομαι (14), ἀκαταστασία (16), ἀνυπόκριτος (17). Chap. iv. μοιχαλίς (4), ὑποτάσσω (7), ἐγγίζω (twice) (8), καθαρίζω (8), ἁμαρτωλός (8), δίψυχος (8), ἐνώπιον (10), καύχησις (16). Chap. v. σητόβρωτος (2), κατιόω (3), ἀφυστερέω (4), σπαταλάω (5), μακροθυμέω (twice) (7), also (8), ἐγγίζω (8), μακροθυμία (10), πολύσπλαγχνος (11), οἰκτίρμων (11), ἐξομολογέω (16), ἁμαρτωλός (20). Here are fifty-two instances and forty-two different words. This is much above the general average. Of these forty-two, twenty-nine are found in the Septuagint, very greatly above the average proportion. It is not difficult to see in this preponderance of the Septuagint vocabulary the position of the author as an untraveled Jew writing to Jews.

The number of late words grouped together in some passages of the New Testament is noticeable; perhaps in no case more so than in the Lord's Prayer. Both Matthew and Luke have ἁγιάζω, ἐπιούσιος, and πειρασμός; Matthew has also θέλημα.

7. A practical inference is derivable from the fact that the late words are formed from the words of the classical period. The one sure and solid preparation, then, that the student needs is a mastery of his Greek classics. It is possible for one who is looking forward to the ministry to flatter himself that he may neglect his college Greek

without much harm to his future course, because the New Testament Greek is peculiar. It will, indeed, seem peculiar to one who enters the theological seminary knowing little of any Greek, and his own performances in it still more peculiar; but one who can read at sight the pages of Xenophon's Memorabilia will find that none of his knowledge is wasted when he opens the Memorabilia of Matthew, Mark, Luke, and John.

INDEXES.

I.—GENERAL INDEX.

	PAGE.
Abba Father, meaning of	185
Acts, revision of by Luke, 131; without Preface, 133; has no word for love	119
Adjectives in -αῖος, how formed and their meaning	67
Ἀγαπάω, meaning of compared with that of φιλέω	115–126
Classical usage	117
Septuagint usage	117
New Testament usage	118
John's usage	120
Alford on the rendering "Evil One" in the Lord's Prayer	85
Alford on the rendering "age" instead of "stature" in Matt. vi. 27	107
Alford on the interval between the writing of Luke and Acts	135
Alford on the "Haven of Crete"	171
Ancient life, the exegete's interest in	14
Apocalypses, extra-canonical, value of	22
Aramaic, was it used in the dialogue in John xxi	122
Aramaic, Paul's use of	81
Aristotle's use of ἀγαπάω and φιλέω	117
Arnold, Matthew, on the Gospel of John	24
Article, Greek, absence of in Luke ii. 14	57

GENERAL INDEX.

	PAGE.
Atonement by self-revelation	152–154
Augustine, St. τοῦ πονηροῦ in the Lord's Prayer	91
Aurelius, M. Antoninus, his "Thoughts"	18
Ballantine on ἀγαπάω and φιλέω	115–117
Barnabas, Epistle of	22
Bengel on ἡλικία	106, 109
Beza's rendering of τοῦ πονηροῦ in the Lord's Prayer	92
Bezal codex as representing the unrevised Acts	131
Bibliotheca Sacra referred to	8, 115, 154, 159, 194
Bi-lingual speech of the Jews	81
Birt on λογος, meaning book	134
Blass on Acts as revised by Luke	131
Blass on the text of Acts xxvi. 28	150
Book-list for New Testament students	43
"Book of the Secrets of Enoch"	22
Burton on the Historical Present	127
Calvin on ἐπιούσιος	63
Chase on ἐπιούσιος	77–79
Chase on the rendering "Evil One" in the Lord's Prayer	84-86, 88
Clementine Homilies, their use of ὁ πονηρός	93
Commentaries, how to use them	42
Concordances, value of	42
Concrete and abstract in the New Testament	85
Coneybeare and Howson on the "Haven of Crete"	172
Consistency, liberal application of in exegesis	33
Cremer's Lexicon on εὐδοκίας	50–53
" " on ἐπιούσιος	59
" " on τοῦ πονηροῦ in Matt. xiii. 38	98
Cureton on the origin of ἐπιούσιος	66

	PAGE.
"Daily" in the Lord's Prayer	83
Deissmann on the Egyptian use of ἀγάπη	195
Demons	113
Demosthenes, ἡλικία in	105
Descent into Hades	137–144
"Didache"	22
Diodorus Siculus	18
Dion Cassius, his use of ἀγαπάω and φιλέω	117
Dionysius, Hal	18
Election	145
Ἡλικία, does it mean "stature" or "age" in Matt. vi. 27?	105–110
Ephrem, Syrus, referred to by Chase	79
Epictetus	18
Ἐπιούσιος in the Lord's Prayer	58–83
" history of its interpretation	58–66
" etymology and meaning	66–73
" renderings of in early versions	73–83
Ernesti on ἐπιούσιος	64
Eternal life, appointment to	145
Evil, or Evil One in the Lord's Prayer	84–104
Evil One (ὁ πονηρός) not the usual term for Devil in the New Testament	96
Exegesis, methods of	39–48
" principles of	25–38
" what it is	27–28
" primary and secondary	28
" has no conflict with science	37
" golden rule of	39
" of other books than the New Testament	47

	PAGE.
Exegesis requires easy sight-reading.	19
Exegete, qualifications of	11–25
Extra-canonical writings	22
Familiar passages, exegesis of	44
Feeling an important element of meaning, 26, 29, 33,	161
Foreknowledge and foreordination	155–158
Gloria in Excelsis discussed.	49–57
Gothic rendering of ἐπιούσιος	73
Grammar, proper use of	45, 160
Greek classics, knowledge of necessary	16
Greek Fathers, value of	22, 92–96
" " on τοῦ πονροῦ in the Lord's Prayer...	91
Greek, post-classical	17
Greek Psalters, light from them on Luke ii. 14	52
Guardian, The, referred to	80
Hades in the New Testament	137–144
Hadley on the speech of the Jews	81
Hall, Isaac H	80
" on the Syriac masculine used for the abstract	90
Harmony, two methods of·	37
Hebraisms	21
Hebraism, is there one in Luke ii. 14?	50
Hebrew and Aramaic, words borrowed from	182–193
Hebrew as illustrating ἐπιούσιος	72
Hebrew words in the Septuagint	191
Herodotus, use of ἡλικία	105
Higher Criticism	23
Hill's Tatian	
Historical Present in the Gospels	127
" " as indicative of authorship	128

GENERAL INDEX.

	PAGE.
History, faculty for in the exegete	14
Human nature, knowledge of in the exegete	15
Hypotheses, value of in exegesis	45
Ideal commands	34
Identity of words	116
Imagination in exegesis	39, 46
Impressions, first, why of value	32
Inerrancy	36
Inspiration	13, 27
James, Epistle of, use of late Greek	199
Jerome on ἐπιούσιος	60
Jerusalem Syriac, rendering of ἐπιούσιος	80
Jesus, origin of the name	192
Jewish Prayer-Book referred to	103
John, quality of his Greek	124
" duplication of words	121, 124
" use of the Historical Present	127
" use of ἀγαπάω and φιλέω	121
" Epistles of, use of ὁ πονηρός	99
" " " ἀγαπάω and φιλέω	121
Josephus 19, use of Hebrew words	192
Kennedy's "Sources of New Testament Greek"	194
Latin, words borrowed from	162–181
" number of	173
" classified	174
" use by different New Testament writers	175
" in Polybius	176
" inferences from	177
" Proper names	178
Lexicon, how to use	42

	PAGE.
Lightfoot, Bishop, on ἐπιούσιος	65, 67, 69, 70
" on τοῦ πονηροῦ	84, 86, 89, 91, 101
Literary features of the New Testament	25
Literature, knowledge of in the exegete	16
Logical power of the exegete	15
Lord's Prayer, ἐπιούσιος in	58–83
" τοῦ πονηροῦ in	84–104
" in Aramaic and Greek	82
" abridged by Luke	88
" late words in	200
Lucian, use of ἡλικία	105
Luke, does his Preface to the Gospel belong also to the Acts?	130–136
Luke, use of ὁ πονηρός, 99; of ἀγαπάω and φιλέω, 119; rare use of the Historical Present	127
Mark, use of ἀγαπάω and φιλέω	119
" free use of the Historical Present	127
Mary, origin of the name	193
Matthew, use of ἀγαπάω and φιλέω	119
" use of the Old Testament	37–101
" use of the Historical Present	127
Meaning made up of thought and feeling	29
" not limited to the apprehension of first hearers	29
" expansion of	29
Meyer on τοῦ πονηροῦ in the Lord's Prayer	85
" on ἡλικιά	107, 109
Meyer, Leo, on ἐπιούσιος	65
Moods and physical condition	44
Murdock's Peshitto Syriac	80

GENERAL INDEX.

	PAGE.
New Testament diction, its relation to the classics	16, 200
" not a mere copy of that of the Septuagint	20, 191, 199
" Kennedy on	194
Old Testament, its help in New Testament exegesis	21
" quotations from, how to interpret	37
Open mind, The, in exegesis	11
Origen on ἐπιούσιος	58
Parables, how explained	35
Paul, origin of his name	179
" use of ἀγαπάω and φιλέω	120
" speech in Aramaic	81
Peter's dialogue with Christ in Aramaic	122
Philo	18
Pliny, Letters of	13
Plutarch, value of	18
" use of ἡλικιά	105
" use of Latin words	178
Polybius, 17; use of Latin words	176
Power of a writing	32
Prayer and exegesis	40
Probation and salvation	146
Problems, exegetical	45
Ramsay's "St. Paul, the Traveler and the Roman Citizen"	130
Ramsay on τὸν πρῶτον λόγον	135
" on Phœnix harbor	171
" on "Saul otherwise Paul"	180
Resurrection of the wicked	142
Resurrection-era	143

GENERAL INDEX.

	PAGE.
Revised Version referred to, 49, 76, 83, 84, 97, 98, 125, 147, 152, 171	
Rhetoric in the New Testament	33
Routine and monotony, to break up	44, 47
Salmasius on ἐπιούσιος	67
Salmon on the authorship of Acts	130
Satan seldom mentioned in the Old Testament	101
Sensitiveness to language	12
Septuagint, value of	20
" use of πονηρόν	100
" of ἡλικία	105
" of ἀγαπάω and φιλέω	117
" of Hebrew and Aramaic words	191
" of words not in the classics	198
Shedd quoted	95
Side-light of another language	41
Silence of New Testament writers	47
Similes in the New Testament	35
Sleeping disciples, Christ's words to	111
Solitary work in exegesis	44
Spirits in prison	141
Spitta's *Apostelgeschichte*	24, 130
Sympathy with the writer	13, 40
Syriac, need of	21
Syriac, Old, Gospels	21
" on ἐπιούσιος	70, 76–83
" on τοῦ πονηροῦ in the Lord's Prayer	90
" on ἡλικιά	110
" rendering of ἀγαπάω and φιλέω	122
Syriac, Peshitto, value of	22

GENERAL INDEX.

	PAGE.
Syriac, rendering of ἀγαπάω and φιλεω	123
Tacitus referred to	13, 164
Talmud on τοῦ πονηροῦ in the Lord's Prayer	102
Tatian's rendering of ἐπιούσιος	79
" of ἡλικία	110
Taylor, Charles, on Tatian, 80; on τοῦ πονηροῦ	91
Textual criticism	23, 26
Thayer's "Books and their Use"	43
" Lexicon	66, 171, 173, 194
Theological inferences in exegesis	159
Tholuck on ἐπιούσιος	63
" on ἡλικία	106
Times, The, relation to New Testament language	25
Tischendorf	23
Traditional interpretations	38
Trench on ἀγαπάω and φιλέω	115
Usage, different kinds and value	30, 31
" distinguish poetic and prose	107
Vincent's "New Testament Handbook"	43
Vischer on Revelation	24
Waiting for light	44, 47
Wendt's "Teaching of Jesus"	24
Westcott and Hort	23, 49
Winer on ἐπιούσιος	67
Woolsey on ἀγαπάω and φιλέω	115, 122
Word-consciousness slight in New Testament	27
Word-study preliminary	41
Words, differences in	106
" relation to general drift	30, 31
" used but once	31

GENERAL INDEX.

                                                                     PAGE.

Words not in classical writers................. 194–201
    " number of, 194, etymological character of 195, rhetorical value 197, doctrinal importance 197, found in the Septuagint 198, in Epistle of James 199, in the Lord's Prayer 200

Wratislaw on ἐπιούσιος.......................... 69

Xenophon's use of the Historical Present.......... 128

Zöckler on the revised Acts.... 131

II.—INDEX OF GREEK WORDS.

	PAGE.		PAGE.
ἀββᾶ	184	δαιμόνιον	113
ἀγαθο–	197	δεισιδαιμονία	198
ἀγαπάω	115-126	δηνάριον	163
ἀγάπη	20, 195, 198	διάβολος	20, 89, 97
ἄγγελος	20	διήγησις	132
ἅγιος	20	δικτάτωρ	177
Ἀΐδης	140	δίψυχος	197
–αῖος	67	Ἑβραϊστί	186
αἰώνιος	41	ἐθελούσιος	70
ἀλληλούϊα	185	εἰδωλολατρεία	199
ἄλφα	184	εἰρήνη	20
ἁμαρτία	89	ἐκ	85
ἁμαρτωλός	20, 198	ἐκκλησία	20
ἀμήν	185, 190	ἐκουῖνος	174
ἀνδρίζω	20	ἐκούσιος	79
ἀνθύπατος	176	Ἑλισάβετ	192
ἀνομία	89	ἐν ὀλίγῳ	150
ἄνωθεν	132	ἐπιοῦσο ἡμέρα	69
ἀπό	85	ἐπιούσιος	58, 83
ἀποκάλυψις	198	ἐπίσκοπος	20
ἀποκύτρωσις	198	ἐργασίαν δοῦναι	147
ἀρραβών	183	ἔρως	198
ἀσσάριον	162	εὐδοκέω	53
ἀφθαροία	198	εὐδοκία	49-57
βάπτισμα -μός -τής	198	εὐραχύλων	173
βάτος	185	ἐφήμερος	75
βῆμα	175	ζηλωτής	20
βουλή	197	ζιζάνιον	190
βυσσός	183	ζωή	20
γέεννα	186, 191, 192	ἡγεμών	175

INDEX OF GREEK WORDS.

	PAGE.
ἡλικία	105-110
θειότης, θεότης	197
θέλημα	197
θεοδίδακτος	197
Ἰησοῦς	192
ἱλασμός, --τήριος	198
Ἰουδαΐζω, --ικῶς	186
Ἰουδαισμός	187
ἰῶτα	184
κακία	89
κάμηλος	183
καρδιογνώστης	197
κεντυρίων	165
κῆνσος	165
κιννάμωμον	183
κοδράντης	165
κολωνία	166
κορβᾶν	187
χορός	187
κόσμος	27
κουστωδία	166
κύμινον	183
κύριος	20
λεγεών	166
λέντιον	166
λίβανος	183
λιβανωτός	184
λιβερτῖνος	173
λίτρα	167
λογομαχία	197

	PAGE.
λόγος	19, 20, 134
λυτρόω	20
μαθητεύω	198, 199
μάκελλον	167
μακροθυμία	197
μαμωνᾶς	187
μάννα	187
μαρὰν ἀθα	188
Μαρία	192
μεμβράνα	167
ἤμ—ἀλλά	87
μίλιον	167
μόδιος	167
μοσχοποιέω	197
ξέστης	168
ὀλίγως	150
ὅσοι	155
ὀφθαλμοδουλεία	197
παλινγεσία	198
πάντοτε	196
παρακολουθέω	135
παῦλος	179
πειράζων, ὁ	89, 97
πείθεις—ποιῆσαι	149
πίστις	20
πληροφορέω	132
πονηρία	89
πονηροῦ, τοῦ	84-104
πραιπόσιτος	174
πραισεντος	174

INDEX OF GREEK WORDS.

	PAGE.		PAGE.
πραιτώριον	168	σπεχονλάτωρ	170
προγιγνώσχω	155	στρατηγός	175
προσάββατον	188	συχάμινος	184
ῥαββί	188	συνείδησις	27, 198, 199
ῥαββουνί	188	σύνψυχος	197
ῥαβδοῦχος	175	τάσσω	145
ῥαχά	189	τίτλος	170
ῥέδη	168	ὕσσωπος	184
ῥῦσαι	85	φαινόλης	170
σαβαώθ	189	φιλέω	115-126
σαββατισμός	189	φίλημα	120
σάββατον	189, 191	ψραγέλλιον -όω	171
σάπφειρος	184	χάρις	20
Σατανᾶς	97	χερουβίμ	190
σάτον	189	χιλίαρχος	175
σιχάριος	168	χριστιανον ποιῆσαι	147
σίχερα	189	χῶρος	171
σιμιχίνθιον	169	ψευδο—	197
σουδάριον	169	ὡσαννά	191

III.—INDEX OF NEW TESTAMENT TEXTS.

(The citations in Sections xvi. and xvii. are not all given.)

MATTHEW.

	PAGE.
ii. 11	184
15	37
iii. 4	183
17	53
iv. 1, 3, 5, 8, 11	89
v. 15	167
22	189
26	166
37	97
41	167
vi. 11	58, 60, 73
13	84, 97
23, 24	86
25-28	107
27	105
33	86
vii. 18	99
23	158
x. 29	163
xii. 24	99
35	30
xiii. 19	97, 99
38	97
xvi. 17	122
xvii. 5	53
12	88
25	165

MATTHEW—Continued.

	PAGE.
xx. 2	164
xxi. 9	190
xxiii. 7	188
15	98
23	183
xxiv. 27	35
xxvi. 45, 46	111
53	166
xxvii. 26	171
27	168
46	182
65	166

MARK.

i. 11	53
ii. 52	106
iv. 15	99
v. 5	74
41	182
vi. 3	37
27	170
45	99
vii. 4	168
11	187
34	182
ix. 47	186
x. 51	189
xii. 30-33	119

INDEX OF NEW TESTAMENT TEXTS.

MARK—Continued.

		PAGE
xiv.	7	74
	36	184
	41	111
xv.	8	74
	34	182
	39	165
	42	188

LUKE.

i.	1-4	130
	15	189
ii.	14	23, 49, 55
iii.	22	53
v.	39	34, 97
vi.	45	97
viii.	12	99
x.	17	113
	18	94
xi.	3	58
	43	119
xii.	22-29	108
	25	105, 107
xvi.	5	186
	7, 9	187
	19	183
xvii.	6	184
xviii.	6	121
xix.	3	109
	20	168

LUKE—Continud.

		PAGE
xix.	38	57
xx.	46	119
xxii.	45, 46	111
	47	119

JOHN.

i.	10	32
	15, 30	124
ii.	15	171
iii.	35	121
v.	2	186
	20	121
	29	143
vi.	37	145, 157
	31	187
ix.	21, 23	106
x.	27	155
xi.	3, 36	121
	11	34
	39	67
xii.	3	167
	25	121
xiii.	4	166
xiv.	2	34
	21	121
xv.	19	121
xvi.	27	121
xvii.	15	97
xix.	19	170
	26	121

JOHN—Continued.

 xx. 2 121
 xxi. 15-17 122

ACTS.

 i. 1, 2 130
  3·12 134
 ii. 27 137
  46 76
 xii. 5 76
 xiii. 9 180
  25 107
  48 145
 xvi. 12 166
 xviii. 11 46
 xix. 12 169
 xx. 28 125
 xxi. 38 169
  40 122
 xxii. 2 81
 xxiv. 15 143
  16 76
 xxvi. 9, 11 159
  28 147
 xxvii. 12 171
 xxviii. 13 67

ROMANS.

 iii. 24-26 152
 viii. 15 184
  29 155

ROMANS—Continued.

 ix. 3 ...... 29, 33, 160
  29 189
 xi. 2 .... 155, 158
 xii. 9, 20, 21 86

1 CORINTHIANS.

 v. 7 188
  13 97
 ix. 17 70
 x. 5 53
  25 167
 xi. 10 45
 xiv. 34 29
 xv. 9 160
  35-38 35
 xvi. 2 189
  15 54
  22 188

2 CORINTHIANS.

 i. 10 85
  20 185
  22 183
 ix. 12 54
 xi. 28 74
 xii. 10 53

GALATIONS.

 i. 13 .... 160, 187
 ii. 14 186
 iii. 16, 20 45
 iv. 6 184

INDEX OF NEW TESTAMENT TEXTS.

EPHESIANS.

	PAGE.
iii. 3	150
iv. 8	137
13	106
27	94
v. 6	98
9	21
vi. 16	97

PHILIPPIANS.

ii. 6-8	20

COLOSSIANS.

i. 13	85

1 THESSALONIANS.

i. 3	76

2 THESSALONIANS.

iii. 3	97

1 TIMOTHY.

v. 5, 23	76

2 TIMOTHY.

ii. 19	158
iv. 7	107
13	167, 171
18	85

TITUS.

iii. 15	120

PHILEMON 14 70

HEBREWS.

	PAGE.
i. 9	120
iv. 9	189
ix. 5	190
19	184
x. 38	53
xi. 11	106
xii. 16	120

JAMES.

i.--iv.	199
i. 12	120
17	21
ii. 5, 8	120
15	75
iv. 7	97
14	35

1 PETER.

i. 8, 22	120
ii. 17	120
iii. 10	120
18-20	141
v. 2	125

2 PETER.

ii. 15	120
18	150

INDEX OF NEW TESTAMENT TEXTS.

1 JOHN.

    ii. 13, 14 97
    iii. 12 .... 97, 98
    v. 18 97
       19 .... 97, 98
       20 98

REVELATIONS.

    i. 5 121
      18 140
    iii. 9, 19 121

REVELATIONS—Contd.

    vi. 8 140
    viii. 3 184
    xii. 11 121
    xviii. 13 168
    xix. 1 185
    xx. 9 121
       13, 14 140
    xxi. 19 184
    xxii. 15 120

www.ingramcontent.com/pod-product-compliance
Lightning Source LLC
Chambersburg PA
CBHW051922160426
43198CB00012B/2004

SAMUEL AND SAUL:

THEIR LIVES AND TIMES.

BY

REV. WILLIAM J. DEANE, M.A.,
RECTOR OF ASHEN, ESSEX.

WIPF & STOCK · Eugene, Oregon

Wipf and Stock Publishers
199 W 8th Ave, Suite 3
Eugene, OR 97401

Samuel and Saul
Their Lives and Times
By Deane, William J.
Softcover ISBN-13: 978-1-7252-9882-8
Hardcover ISBN-13: 978-1-7252-9883-5
eBook ISBN-13: 978-1-7252-9884-2
Publication date 1/29/2021
Previously published by Anson D. F. Randolph and Co., 1889

This edition is a scanned facsimile of
the original edition published in 1889.